Mountain Bike Adventures in

WASHINGTON'S
SOUTH CASCADES
AND PUGET SOUND

SECOND EDITION

TOM KIRKENDALL

THE
MOUNTAINEERS

Published by
The Mountaineers
1001 SW Klickitat Way
Seattle, Washington 98134

09876
54321

Published simultaneously in Canada by Douglas & McIntyre, Ltd., 1615 Venables Street, Vancouver, B.C. V5L 2H1

Published simultaneously in Great Britain by Cordee, 3a DeMontfort Street, Leicester, England, LE1 7HD

Printed in Canada

Edited by Dana Fos
Maps by the author
All photographs by Kirkendall/Spring Photographers
Cover design by Watson Graphics
Book design and layout by Gray Mouse Graphics

Cover photograph: *Mt. Rainier dominates the skyline at Sun Top Lookout.*
Frontispiece: *Rider on Hamilton Butte (Route 44)*

Library of Congress Cataloging-in-Publication Data
Kirkendall, Tom.
    Mountain bike adventures in Washington's South Cascades and Puget Sound / Tom Kirkendall. — 2nd ed.
      p.   cm.
    Includes index.
    ISBN 0-89886-414-3
    1. Bicycle touring—Washington (State)—Guidebooks. 2. All terrain bicycles. 3. Bicycle trails—Washington (State)—Guidebooks. 4. Bicycle touring—Washington (State)—Puget Sound—Guidebooks. 5. Bicycle touring—Cascade Range—Guidebooks. 6. Puget Sound (Wash.)—Guidebooks. 7. Cascade Range—Guidebooks. 8. Washington (State)—Guidebooks. I. Title.
GV1045.5.W2K58   1996
796.6'0979—dc20
                                     96–12034
                                        CIP

Contents

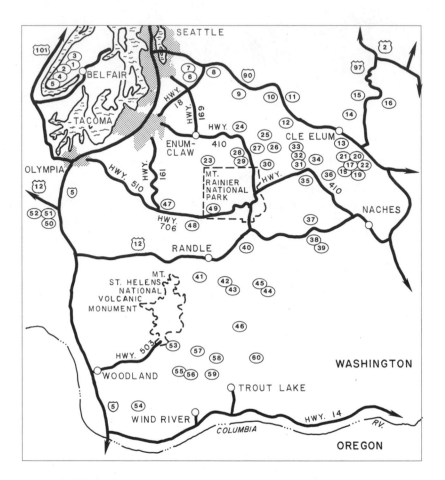

Highway 12—West

Mt. Rainier—West

Capitol Forest

Mount St. Helens

Vancouver

Wind River

Trout Lake

Index   219

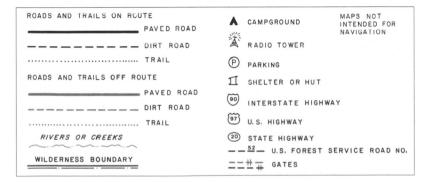

The guidebook didn't say the water was going to be this cold!

A Note about Safety

Safety is an important concern in all outdoor activities. No guidebook can alert you to every hazard or anticipate the limitations of every reader. Therefore, the descriptions of roads, trails, routes, and natural features in this book are not representations that a particular place or excursion will be safe for your party. When you follow any of the routes described in this book, you assume responsibility for your own safety. Under normal conditions, such excursions require the usual attention to traffic, road and trail conditions, weather, terrain, the capabilities of your party, and other factors. Because many of the lands in this book are subject to development and/or change of ownership, conditions may have changed since this book was written that make your use of some of these routes unwise. Always check for current conditions, obey posted private property signs, and avoid confrontations with property owners or managers. Keeping informed on current conditions and exercising common sense are the keys to a safe, enjoyable outing.

The Mountaineers

Evans Creek (Route 23)

Introduction

Wheels, Gravel, and You—Part 2

Since the first edition of this book, published in 1989, a lot has changed in the world of mountain biking. At that time, mountain biking was a relatively new sport, with only a small number of truly serious riders. Times have changed and the joys of mountain bike riding are now savored by many.

When the first riders rolled out onto the trails it seemed to forest managers and to the cyclists themselves that mountain bikes were environmentally pure, without the noise and exhaust of an ORV and without the appetite for delicate alpine meadows and the phenomenal ability to create waste products of a horse. Motorcycle trails are known for their deep ruts caused by the high-powered skidding of wheels on steep climbs. Horse trails are churned to dust bowls or muddy swamps by the sharp hooves. In fact, the wide tires and relatively light weight of the mountain bikes and their riders lulled us into believing that we could not cause damage to the trails the way motorcycles and horses do. It initially seemed that mountain bikes would be less destructive to trails than hikers who must centralize their weight on two feet rather than spread it out over a 26-by-2-inch tire surface.

Well guess what . . . just like hikers, horses, and ORVs, mountain bikes do leave evidence of their passing. Trails that used to be smooth are now rutted by enthusiastic riders using improper braking techniques and riding styles.

Up to this point, most of us have spent all our time looking forward. Now it is time to start looking backward and checking for skid marks and ruts. Watch yourself at corners and avoid jamming on the back brake to skid around a turn. That skid is the start of a rut, and a rut is the start of the breakdown of the trail.

Keep a light touch when riding in damp areas. Did you leave a rut? Let's start thinking environmental impact . . . which means leaving no trace of our passing. Obviously, some soils are more prone to hold moisture than others. Look at each trail as you go. Certain trails are not suitable for riding when the soil is damp . . . so wait until the soil dries out before riding there.

Puddles pose a more difficult dilemma. There is no way to ride through a puddle without enlarging the problem. The only solution is to call for a total moral ban against splashing through puddles like a happy three-year-old. And, of course, it won't solve anything if you increase the size of the trail by simply riding around the puddle. The only environmentally friendly way to deal with a puddle is to get off your bike and push it through the wet area while you walk around the edge or, even better, to carry the bike until you are back on solid, dry trail.

The final step is for all riders to share in repairing the damage. It's time to spend a day on a trail crew. Call your local DNR (Department of Natural Resources), Forest Service, or Washington Trails Association (206) 517-7032 to find out about the all-volunteer trail crews in your area.

Knobby Rules
(The Mountain Biker's Emily Post)

One book cannot cover every possible mountain bike ride, nor would ten books. The aim is to introduce you, the rider, to as many areas and as wide a variety of terrain as possible in the limited space available.

With all these places to ride it is easy to forget that there are some areas where mountain bike riding is neither legal nor acceptable. Mountain bikes are not allowed on trails in Mt. Rainier

Rule #2: Leave no trace.

National Park. No bicycles are allowed in any of the National Forest Wilderness Areas, as stipulated in the Wilderness Act of 1964: "There shall be no form of mechanical transport . . . in any such area." Mountain bikes are not allowed on "Hiker Only" trails, which generally receive this designation because they are either too short, too crowded, or too boggy for riding. The entire Pacific Crest Trail is closed to mountain bikes from Mexico to Canada. The final restrictions to watch out for are seasonal road and trail closures. When the Forest Service gates or closes a road, mountain bikes are welcome. When the county or private landowners close a road, get permission before entering the area. Seasonal closures on trails apply to mountain bikes, as the wheels may cause ruts in soft, wet ground.

As mountain biking is clearly the newest entry into the crowded field of outdoor recreation, riders must work to gain the acceptance and respect of the traditional forest and trail users. Thanks to a few irresponsible riders, thousands of miles of trails have been closed to mountain bikes. Do your part to maintain access by observing the following rules formulated by the International Mountain Bicycling Association (IMBA). IMBA's mission and my own is to promote environmentally sound and socially responsible mountain biking.

1. **Ride on open trails.** Respect trail and road closures (ask if not sure), avoid possible trespass on private land, obtain permits and authorization as may be required. Federal and state wilderness are areas closed to cycling. The way you ride will influence trail management decisions and policies.
2. **Leave no trace.** Be sensitive to the dirt beneath you. Even on open (legal) trails, you should not ride under conditions where you will leave evidence of your passing, such as on certain soils after a rain. Recognize different types of soils and trail construction; practice low-impact cycling. This also means staying on existing trails and not creating any new ones. Be sure to pack out at least as much as you pack in.
3. **Control your bicycle.** Inattention for even a second can cause problems. Obey all bicycle speed regulations and recommendations.
4. **Always yield trail.** Make known your approach well in advance. A friendly greeting (or bell) is considerate and works well; don't startle others. Show your respect when passing by slowing to a walking pace or even stopping (always stop if there are children present). Anticipate other trail users around corners or blind spots.
5. **Never spook animals.** All animals are startled by an unannounced approach, a sudden movement, or a loud noise. This can be dangerous for you, others, and the animals. Give animals

extra room and time to adjust to you. When passing horses use special care and follow directions from the horseback riders (ask if uncertain). Running cattle and disturbing wildlife are a serious offensees. Leave gates as you found them, or as marked.

6. **Plan ahead.** Know your equipment, your ability, and the area in which you are riding—and prepare accordingly. Be self-sufficient at all times, keep your equipment in good repair, and carry necessary supplies for changes in weather or other conditions. A well-executed trip is a satisfaction to you and not a burden or offense to others. Always wear a helmet.

Most hikers and horse riders do not mind sharing trails with mountain bikes because they travel quietly. Unfortunately, it is that wonderful silence that makes the mountain bike a potential hazard on the trail. Hikers cannot hear an approaching bicycle and horses are spooked far beyond the limited reach of their brains when suddenly faced with a mechanical imitation of themselves. Add speed to the bicycle's silent approach, and hikers have no time to react, while horses may go into a panic that endangers both them and their riders.

Nobody wants to be the cause of an accident or serious injury, so ride intelligently. If you can't see what is around a bend or

Ouch! This is not low-impact cycling.

switchback, then slow down to a speed that allows you to stop abruptly if necessary. If any problem arises it is up to you, the silent and unseen newcomer on the trail, to pull off to the side for hikers bent under heavy, cumbersome packs; to hide behind a tree when a horse refuses to walk past your mechanical steed; and to pick up the bike and move around the heavier motorcycles on a steep and narrow trail.

The way to avoid accidents is simple: use common sense, make your presence known, and SLOW DOWN. Using common sense is easy—just ride with your brain engaged. Making your presence known requires ingenuity. Yell, sing, talk, shout, or put cards in your spokes; it does not matter how you do it, just be sure you're noticed. Slowing down is the most difficult thing for a cyclist to do, even though it is only a matter of an extra pull on the brakes. However, when you can't see the trail ahead, the only way to ensure your safety and the safety of other trail users is to SLOW DOWN.

Silence is also a problem when cycling on logging roads. When you hear a vehicle coming towards you, remember that the driver can't hear you, so get out of the way. Avoid accidents by rounding every corner as if there might be a cow, car, or logging truck on the other side. Do not ride in a group on corners—always ride single file on the correct side of the road.

Use some common sense, make your presence known, slow down when you cannot see ahead, and have a great ride.

Heading Out into the Woods

This is a *where*-to-ride book, so do not look any further here to find *how* to ride. However, a few words of advice are offered in the following pages.

Equipment

The Bike: Mountain bikes are changing radically each year, with stronger, more durable components, lighter frames, novel suspension arrangements, and different frame angles. As long as their development continues at full steam, any attempt here to describe the perfect mountain bike would be counterproductive. Before going shopping, do some homework. Read catalogs and magazines that specialize in mountain bikes and study the bike reviews and prices.

When you are ready to purchase that new bike, go shopping with a heavy wallet. The quality of the mountain bike you purchase is directly related to the amount of money spent, up to around $1,200. (This is a figure for 1996 and is expected to rise.) Low-end

I hope the rider was wearing a helmet.

bikes are sufficient for paved road use, with poor-quality frames and inexpensive components that will require both time and extra money to keep in working order. Bikes starting around $700 are a good bet for a first purchase. The frame quality of these bikes is good and the components very durable. As components wear out on the midrange bikes they are easy to replace.

If you are not a competent bicycle mechanic yourself, the next step is to look around for a good shop to do your repairs. Your mechanic is as important as your bike, and finding a skilled one can make the difference in how long the bike will last and how safe the bike is out in the woods. If your mechanic is especially good, ensure his or her continued interest in your bike by occasionally stopping in just to say thanks or to deliver a six-pack of a favored beverage.

Helmet: If you do not already own a helmet, stop reading and go out and buy one. Spills and tumbles on a mountain bike are far more common than on a touring or street bike.

Glasses: Ride with some kind of eye protection at all times.

16

Bugs and dirt in the eyes are common experiences for riders without glasses and very difficult to dig out when speeding down a mountain road.

Gloves: If you now ride without gloves, acquire a pair immediately. Gloves not only cushion your hands from shock on the handle bars, they also protect the sensitive palms of the hands from abrasions when you fall.

Clothing: What you wear when you ride is pretty much a matter of personal choice. Some riders prefer shiny, skin-tight outfits in brilliant colors that put an alpine meadow to shame. Others dress in earthy old shorts and holey T-shirts. Experiment with your wardrobe, then take your choice. Generally whatever is already in your wardrobe for cycling or hiking will work. The only stipulation is to avoid loose, baggy shirts, shorts, or pants that may catch on any part of the bike when you're riding.

Be sure to carry enough clothing for any situation. This is Washington and it can rain on any day it pleases. In the mountains, July rains can turn into July snows requiring hats, gloves, long underwear, and rain suits. And on any rainy day the clouds can suddenly disappear and leave you sweltering in the sunshine.

Shoes: There are special shoes on the market designed to protect the foot and ankle as well as to give a solid grip on the pedal. For starters any shoe that is comfortable to walk in and has a sole stiff enough to protect the foot from the lumps and spurs of the pedal will suffice.

Toe-clips and Clipless Pedals: The toughest decision to make when buying your first mountain bike is what kind of pedals to buy. As this issue can be debated to eternity, do not look for an answer here. I suggest that, on your first few attempts at trail riding, you ride with standard old pedals rather than clipless pedals or pedals with toe-clips. This will encourage you to learn to use your feet to save yourself from falls. Once feet-saves become part of your riding, add clipless pedals or toe-clips that are specially designed for mountain-bike riding.

Clipless pedals are very comfortable, extremely convenient, and less bulky than toe-clips, but they do have a couple of disadvantages. When shoes are set up for clipless pedals they can be difficult to walk in. It also takes a little longer to get out of clipless pedals, a definite disadvantage when riding through mud or on snow.

Cycle Computer: A small cycle computer, mounted on your handle bars, will help in following the directions given in the log section of each ride. The computer should be water-resistant or waterproof.

Bike Bag or Pack: In order to carry the vast array of clothing needed to greet any situation, it is best to have a large fanny pack,

Valley Trail—North and South

a small knapsack, or a pack that fits on the top of the back wheel rack. Avoid panniers like a plague unless you are planning an overnight trip. Pannier bags will be ripped to shreds in the brush, bounce off the rack on rough roads, or catch on branches and flip you off your bike.

Water: Equip your bike with as many large-size water bottles as the frame will allow. Never drink water found along the route. If you cannot carry enough water on your bike, stick an extra quart in your gear or carry a water filter.

Tire Repair Kit: Flat tires occur even in the woods, so be sure to equip your bike with a patch kit and a good pump. There are pumps on the market specially designed for mountain bikes, which are very nice. These pumps are short to fit the smaller mountain frames, are thicker than regular pumps to move a large quantity of air quickly back into the fat tires, and have covers to keep the pump head clean.

Bicycle Repair Kit: Carry a repair kit that is equipped to do at least a minimum of repairs in the woods. Always carry a valve stem tightener, a chain tool, 5- and 6-mm Allen wrenches, a spare brake cable and derailleur cable, a foldable cable spoke, and a small roll of tape for everything else. To these supplies add the tools needed to take off a wheel, remove a tire, and replace a broken cable. (If you do not know what tools are needed for your bike, roll it into a bike shop and ask.) If you are riding with a large group or have some extra room, add a spare rear derailleur and a few extra chain links, as well as a crank tool, head set and bottom bracket wrench, open-end wrenches, a spoke wrench, and a few extra screws for racks, water bottles, and shift levers. For the problems you can't repair, carry a 5- to 10- foot section of cord to tow home a companion with a busted pedal or crank. No matter how prepared you are, some problems will force even the most experienced to walk home, such as a broken rim, a busted crank arm, or a broken fork. So be as prepared as possible and save the tales of the really bad trips to be written up and submitted to a magazine that specializes in incredible odysseys.

First-aid Kit: The subject of bicycle repair leads directly to the subject of body repair. Spills are frequent when riding and riders seem to spend a lot of time comparing bruises and scrapes. If helmet and gloves are worn, falls are rarely serious. However, it is essential to be prepared. Carry a small and compact first-aid kit on all rides. This kit should have a large roll of tape and numerous large gauze pads for abrasions as well as butterfly bandages for deep cuts. Carry several cravats for strapping up sprained or broken extremities. Bugs can be a problem at any time and repellent is often very handy. In the late summer be prepared for bees. If sensitive to stings, talk to your doctor and carry the proper

Stringers become well embedded at 20 mph.

medicine. Bees seem to resent being run into by speeding cyclists and are very demonstrative about it.

Food: The last item, because you will wish to pack it on top, is the food. There are no convenience stores out in the woods, so carry lots of everything to contend with that famous cycling appetite.

Physical Condition

Mountain bike riding is an extremely physically demanding sport. Before starting out on your first ride of the season put in plenty of miles on an indoor wind trainer and a lot of miles on the road. Remember that the energy expended on a 50-mile ride on paved road is equivalent to about 12 miles on a rough, steep mountain road or trail. All other forms of active exercise will add to overall fitness so, if time or inclination allows, cross-country ski in the winter, follow a weight training program, or jog frequently.

Bike Condition

Consider your mountain bike an extension of your own body and make sure it is in good condition also. Before each ride do a quick check of the bike. Check for nuts, bolts, or screws that may

It's a long walk back home when you have a broken derailleur and no repair kit.

have rattled loose. Check the head set and bottom bracket and make sure they feel tight. If in doubt about how this is done, take a class, buy a book or a video, and even if you never do your own maintenance at least learn the symptoms of all problems.

Caution—Guidebook Ahead

The mountain bike routes in this book have been detailed as accurately as possible. However, all of the rides in this book are unprotected and subject to change. Good roads are abandoned when all the timber is cut in an area, and old roads are reopened and covered with a slippery layer of uncrushed gravel. Trails may be cut by new roads and logging clearings, signs taken down or stolen, and the tread covered by slides or massive blow-downs.

Info

Roads and trails may be closed at any time during the year due to logging activity, slides, fire hazard, or weather. Calling ahead is the best way to make sure that the route you wish to ride will be open. To help you obtain the most up-to-date information before you leave home, the "Info" listing in the block at the top of each route description notes where this kind of information may be obtained for that route.

In the following list you will find the phone numbers for each of the agencies listed in the "Info" section. In most cases, information is available during business hours, weekdays only. Four different phone numbers are listed for the DNR. The first is a toll-free number to the state office in Olympia. You may call this number and ask to be connected with any of the seven area offices in the state without charge. The next three DNR listings refer to specific area offices. The other abbreviation used in the list is RS, which stands for Ranger Station. In several cases I was unable to find any source of information for the route; embark on these rides with a sense of adventure.

Cle Elum RS (509) 674-4411

DNR 1-800-527-3305

DNR (Castle Rock) (360) 577-2025

DNR (Chehalis) (360) 748-8616

DNR (Ellensburg) (509) 925-6131

DNR (Enumclaw) (206) 825-1631

Lake Easton State Park (Iron Horse State Park) (509) 656-2586

Mt. Adams RS (509) 395-2501

Mt. Rainier National Park (360) 569-2211

Mount St. Helens National Volcanic Monument (360) 274-5473

Mt. Tahoma Ski Trails Association (360) 569-2451 (mid-December–March, Saturday and Sunday only)

Naches RS (509) 653-2205

Pack Forest (206) 832-6534

Packwood RS (360) 494-5515

Randle RS (360) 497-7565

Weyerhaeuser (Snoqualmie) (206) 888-4250

White River RS (206) 825-2571

Wind River RS (509) 427-5645

Maps

Finding a good map that keeps up to date with new roads and trail changes is a real challenge. In the block at the beginning of each trail description is the recommended map for the trip. In

Volunteers working in conjunction with the Forest Service to find new routes for mountain bikers near Tacoma Pass

choosing a map for each trip I checked several sources to determine which map best showed the route. Unfortunately, in some areas accurate maps are simply not available.

The criteria I used for maps were the following: (1) all roads and trails cycled should be represented on the map and (2) maps should have contour lines or some system to show the topography of the area.

Below is a listing of maps recommended in the route descriptions with a brief summary of features and problems:

Green Trails: Topographic maps with trails highlighted in green. These maps are easy to read and use a 15-minute base, which is good enough for all navigation on roads and trails. They are not updated very often and frequently are out of date. Also, they do not show all the old, abandoned railroad grades. Green Trails maps do not cover any areas beyond the heartland of the Cascade and Olympic Ranges.

USGS Maps: Excellent topographic maps published by the Geodetic Survey. These maps now come in the 7.5-minute format, which means they are unequaled for off-road and off-trail route finding, but the area covered by each sheet is so small you will

Not all trails are as easy to follow as this one (Route 15). Always carry a good map.

often find that multiple maps are required for a simple ride. At the time of this publication the USGS maps were all moderately up to date in terms of roads and trails.

Metsker County Maps: A thorough coverage of all roads, trails, lakes, and rivers for each county in the state of Washington. These are excellent maps for locating roads but lack names and numbers on secondary roads. The maps are white with blue or black print and so full of detail that they can be hard to read. No contours are given, and no feeling for the local terrain is conveyed.

National Forest Road and Trail Maps: Cover an entire forest, showing the roads and trails that are currently being maintained. These maps are very helpful for locating campgrounds and trailheads but inadequate for detailed route finding.

Ranger District Maps: Wonderful maps that cover an entire ranger district. Although by no means perfect, they are the most accurate maps available. The main disadvantage of these maps is that they are huge and easily ripped. The maps are available from the individual ranger district offices as well as the forest headquarter offices for a very reasonable price.

Free Maps: Numerous maps can be obtained for free by writing. Weyerhaeuser offers several helpful Recreation and Hunting

Maps. Write to 7001 396th SW, Snoqualmie, WA 98065 for the Snoqualmie and White River tree farms; P.O. Box 540, Chehalis, WA 98532 for the Vail and McDonald tree farms; and P.O. Box 188, Longview, WA 98632 for the St. Helens West map. Maps are available from Pack Forest (see Route 47) by writing to Pack Forest, 9010 453rd Street East, Eatonville, WA 98328 or by calling (206) 832-6534 weekdays. You may also pick up a map in person from the main office in the Administration Center at Pack Forest.

DNR Maps: Good maps of trails and roads in Capitol Forest, Tahuya, and Yacolt Burn (Jones Creek) State Forests, are available by writing to the Department of Natural Resources, 1065 South Capitol Way AW-11, Olympia, WA 98504. Finally, also from DNR, a booklet showing all the ORV areas in the entire state of Washington may be obtained by writing the above address.

Mileage

In the description of each ride is a mileage log, keyed to important landmarks, turning points, or attractions along the way. The miles were recorded with a cycle computer and are as accurate as possible, which is something less than 100 percent. If you do not get the same mileages on your computer, do not be disturbed. Mentally insert two words before each log entry: "At about." To aid in your route finding I have added elevations (in parentheses) at most of the major intersections.

Whereas I would very much like to be informed by users of this book about changes or corrections in the text, I have no desire to make a comparison of the idiosyncrasies of all the cycle computers on the market.

Description

The description section of each block gives a *very* brief synopsis of the type of riding involved and the difficulties encountered. The routes are noted as being on road, trail, or road and trail.

Roads (also called double tracks) fall under several categories:

Well maintained—the surface is in good condition.

Abandoned—probably rough in some sections; trees may not be cut out, streams or water bars may cut across the road, bridges may not be in good condition, and 4-wheeled vehicles cannot travel the entire length.

Railroad grade—roads that follow abandoned railroad lines, climbing very gradually or not at all.

4×4 routes—a wide category of roads formally called jeep roads, driveable only by vehicles with high clearance and 4-wheel drive. The condition of these roads varies from good to impassable. Most 4×4 routes are steep, deeply rutted, and challenging to ride.

Steep—requiring considerable effort to ride.

Steep in sections—the road is not steep for the entire distance.

Rough—loose rocks or gravel on the road, or bedrock sticking out of the surface. Parts of these roads may be very difficult to ride up. Expect to be bounced and jarred on the descent.

Rough in sections—roads whose surface varies.

Trails (also known as single tracks) use much of the same terminology as roads. Additional terms are the following:

ORV trail—designed for motorcycles. Many have banked corners and are fun to ride.

ATV trail—designed for the three- and 4-wheel motorbikes. These trails are wide and easy to ride, great for beginning off-road mountain biking.

Sandy—difficult to ride up and requiring caution and skill when descending.

Steep—steeper grades than found on *steep* roads. When the term *steep* is used to describe a trail, expect to push your bike some or all of the way up.

Well graded—strong bikers can ride most of the way up.

Roads *and* **Trails:** When the description notes *road and trail* you can expect the roads to be used mostly for the ascent and trails for the descent.

Rating

Each trip is rated for difficulty as follows:

Easy—this category includes only well-maintained mountain roads, a rare trail or two, and railroad grades with little elevation gain. No previous mountain biking experience is necessary to enjoy the ride.

Moderate—rides in this category are on roads and trails. The roads may be steep in sections, rocky, poorly maintained, or abandoned. The trails in this category are generally well maintained.

If the route exceeds your ability, walking is a healthy alternative.

Skilled—rough terrain, strenuous climbs, and steep descents characterize the roads and trails in this category. Skilled trips require considerable energy and experience.

Adventurous—routes in this category are designed to challenge skilled riders. These rides may require bushwhacking or route finding, and/or they may follow roads or trails that are not maintained and are extremely steep and very rough.

How to Choose a Ride

The rides in this guidebook vary from easy to very difficult. To find a route that will challenge but not surpass your skills, check out the information block provided at the beginning of each route description. Start off by checking the trip rating, then compare the trip mileage with the elevation gain. Finally, read the short description describing the roads and trails found on the route. If the route sounds interesting, go ahead and check through the more detailed description given in the text.

Once under way, if the chosen route turns out to be too difficult for anyone in your group, including yourself, recognize your limitations and turn around. If you find yourself in an uncomfortable position, remember that you can always get off your bicycle and walk.

Stop! Read This

A mountain biker never heads up a trail planning to run over a hiker, scare a little child, or cause a horse to throw its rider. It's a matter of public record, however, that mountain bikes have hit hikers, startled children, and caused steeds to toss their riders. So before you mount your bike and head for the trails, please hear me out as I mount the soapbox. With a little consideration and cooperation, maybe we can prevent other wilderness users from viewing us as pariahs.

Nowhere in the Constitution is it written, "We the people allow mountain bikers to go wherever they please," nor does it read, "Life, liberty, and the pursuit of happy mountain biking." The facts are simple: We have no ordained rights. In fact, because we are new to the recreational scene, we are lowest on the totem pole.

As newcomers, it's very easy for us to tread on the toes of pre-existing users—a practice that will see ever-increasing numbers of signs reading, "No mountain bikers allowed."

Uncrowded riding opportunities exist close to all major population centers in this state. So why do we insist on riding in areas crawling with pedestrians? Convenience is a poor answer.

What part of "No" don't you understand?

Take the city parks for example. Sure, they are only a couple of miles from home and they are crammed with trails. Just the ticket for some fun, right? Wrong. Just the ticket to hit a walker or run over a child. Just the ticket to create the image for our group that unscrupulous lawyers have created for theirs.

Remember, you are riding a *mountain* bike, not a *city park* bike. The park system was developed for pedestrians who need areas where they can stroll, free from buses, cars, motorbikes, and— yes—mountain bikes.

Okay, unless you're really dim, you're getting the idea now. Take your mountain bike to the mountains. But don't take it to the heavily used hiking trails or you'll create the same good will you mustered in the city parks. This is especially true if the trail is signed "Hiker Only." Hikers struggled long and hard for the creation of such trails. They struggled with the government to protect these areas from fast-moving motorcycles so they could walk safely with their families. In some areas (the Issaquah Alps is an excellent example) hikers donated their time and energy to build their own trails so that they would have a place to walk in peace. So leave them in peace.

Find your own space. This book is designed to give you ideas about where to find such space, but it is amazingly incomplete. Look around. You'll find numerous areas to ride around the fringes of every city or town in this state. Search your maps for Off-Road Vehicle (ORV) Trails, abandoned railroad grades, and powerline or pipeline right of ways. Check out old maps for abandoned county roads or logging roads. You'll discover gems forgotten by everyone.

One last pitch while I'm preaching. I believe mountain bikers should start earning their "right" to ride. It's time for us to stake our own claims rather than rob the gold mined by others. It's time for groups of riders to work with city, county, and state administrations, as well as local hiking groups, to determine where rarely used or abandoned trails could be set aside as mountain bike trails. Ask the same questions of federal agencies that have lands nearby.* If riders are willing to devote the necessary leg and arm work, we may soon have our own areas with signs reading, "Mountain Bike Trail."

Until then, let's channel our energies into riding in places where we will not annoy or endanger others.

---

*For example, to find out about the Department of Natural Resources (DNR) lands in your area call 1-800-562-6010. Inquire about their nearby lands, then study the usage of these lands. If you find an area with little use, develop a plan and submit it to the DNR.

Wow, what a great ride!

1. Looped in Tahuya

Loop trip: 20.0 miles
Elevation gain: 180 feet
Map: Tahuya State Forest Map
Best: all year
Allow: 4–6 hours

Description: ORV trail (loose
   rock and roots); road (rough
   4×4 routes with giant potholes)
Rating: skilled
Info: DNR (South Puget Sound)

Tahuya State Forest, located on the southern end of the Kitsap Peninsula, is a grand place to ride, with ORV trails to challenge you, miles of 4×4 routes to further challenge you, and miles of roads to escape to when you have had enough challenges.

Tahuya State Forest is a lowland cut by deep creeks and rivers and dotted with lakes and marshes in shallow basins. Timber grows excellently here and the trails wind through tree farms as well as second-growth forest. In spring the flowers bloom, a curious mixture of skunk cabbage, trilliums, and lilies. Near the end of May the forest blossoms out with a tremendous display of native rhododendrons. In the fall the leaves of the northern black birch trees create a colorful display along the rivers.

Looped in Tahuya is a ride that takes advantage of the network of 4×4 routes and ORV trails. This route follows official DNR-sanctioned routes, but you will pass miles of unofficial trails which create a maze that can be hard to unravel. The official routes are marked with signs or diamonds (gray, blue, or orange) at most junctions.

Access: Drive to the town of Belfair at the tip of Hood Canal and follow signs towards Belfair State Park. Turn west on NE

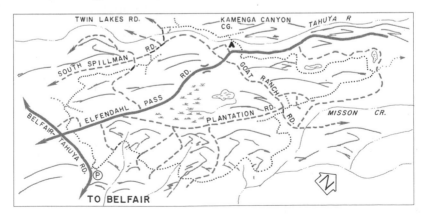

31

Clifton Lane for 0.2 mile to a 4-way intersection. Go straight on Highway 300 West (also called North Shore Road) for 3.5 miles. (Belfair State Park, passed at 3.1 miles, has restrooms and water.) Take a right on Belfair–Tahuya Road and head uphill for 1.1 miles to the Mission Creek Trailhead located on the right side of the road. Park here (470 feet).

MILEAGE LOG

0.0 Before taking off, take time to look back the way you came. From the parking area entrance, Mt. Rainier stands bold over the southeastern horizon. This is the best view of the loop; enjoy, then head into the forest. Two trails begin from this trailhead. You should start out on the Mission Creek Trail, the one on the right. You will return to this point by the trail on the left.

At the time of this writing the Mission Creek Trail was in excellent condition, well marked, and easy to follow. The only intersections noted here will be the ones where you might get confused. Enjoy your ride.

Yahoo! We're having fun!

1.4 The trail reaches a well-maintained forest road and ends temporarily. Go right for 20 feet then find the trail again on your left.

2.9 The trail merges with a road. Go left following the road for 500 feet then turn right to return to the trail (370 feet). In this next section you will pass by several logging clearings then arrive at a large trail map in the middle of nowhere. Go left and head back into the forest.

7.1 Intersection, stay to the left and continue to follow the Mission Creek Trail.

7.5 Cross Goat Ranch Road. The trail heads through a band of trees and then across a tree plantation.

7.6 Two trails join at the edge of the plantation. Go right along the edge of the old cut, ignoring all spur roads and trails.

8.3 The trail divides; go right across a bridge, then immediately turn left. The trail continues north, passing a second bridge then a small lake, both on your left.

9.1 Just beyond the lake there is a 4-way intersection. Go left (west), heading over Tahuya Ridge towards Kamenga Canyon on the Overland Trail.

9.2 The trail briefly joins a road. Go left for 75 feet then take a right back on the trail.

10.4 On the west side of Tahuya Ridge the trail divides several times as it crosses over the top of an old clearcut. Stay left, following the newly rerouted trail through the forest.

11.2 At this "Y" junction go left; at the next stay right. The trail heads across a hillside crisscrossed with old roads, old trails, and unofficial routes. Follow the diamond trail markers carefully.

11.6 Go right on an old road and spend the next 0.5 mile heading north along the valley floor. The trail winds through the trees crossing several roads and spur trails.

12.1 Cross the paved Elfendahl Pass Road then head into dense forest.

12.4 Go straight across a road then cycle along a bench overlooking the small Kamenga Canyon Campground. At the southern end of the camp, descend a steep path, then ride across the Tahuya River on a wooden bridge. The trail divides here; go straight on the Tahuya River Trail, which follows the river south.

13.2 The trail divides; go to the right, uphill into the trees. The trail on the left descends to a historical marker commemorating the site of Camp Spillman, a World War II firefighting camp.

13.3 Intersection; go left for 20 feet on an old road then rejoin the trail on the right.

13.8 The trail reaches Twin Lakes Road. Turn left and cycle across the Tahuya River and past the Tahuya River Trail.

14.0 Go right on nearly level, gravel-surfaced South Spillman Road.

14.4 When the road begins to climb, go left on a narrow, unmarked 4×4 road. After heading uphill for 200 feet go right on the official 4×4 route and head south. Although this route is well marked with diamonds, it is not always easy to pick out which of the multiple spurs will keep you out of the deepest mud pits. Weave your way through this braided maze of roads as best you can and use caution when heading across any mud hole.

14.9 The 4×4 route ends temporarily at East Tahuya Spur Road. Go right for 500 feet then left to return to mud-puddle hopping.

17.0 The 4×4 route bends east.

17.8 The 4×4 route skims along the edge of the Tahuya River Trail for 20 feet. Leave the road and go left onto the trail.

18.7 The trail crosses a dirt road.

19.1 Use caution to cross paved, and occasionally busy, Elfendahl Pass Road.

20.0 The Tahuya River Trail and this loop end at the Mission Creek Trailhead.

KITSAP PENINSULA

2. Tahuya River Loop

Loop trip: 20.1 miles
Elevation gain: 250 feet
Map: Tahuya State Forest Map
Best: all year
Allow: 4–6 hours

Description: ORV trail; loose rocks, tree roots, and some steep sections
Rating: skilled
Info: DNR (South Puget Sound)

The Tahuya River Loop is ideal for perfecting your riding skills. On this route through the Tahuya State Forest you will encounter sections of loose rocks, tree roots, steep descents, puddles, ruts, and sand traps. Despite the challenges, the ride is not just an obstacle course. There are sections of trail where you relax and enjoy gliding through fern-covered gullies, cruising beside a marsh, or cranking down a straightaway.

The best time to ride this loop is in spring, fall, or winter, when there is less ORV noise and competition. The spring is particularly nice as the forest flowers bloom (skunk cabbage, trillium, and Oregon grape in April and a brilliant display of native rhododendrons in late May). Fall color brightens the forest along the rivers and marshes where the birch trees grow, making autumn especially beautiful (watch out for hunters), and winter is quiet as the puddles and lakes ice over.

Access: Drive to the Mission Creek Trailhead (470 feet) as described in Route 1.

MILEAGE LOG

0.0 Before leaving the parking area, pedal over to the entrance and check out the view of Mt. Rainier. Next head to the upper end of the parking area and find the two trails that start there. For this ride you want the Tahuya River Trail, which starts on the left and heads east through the forest.

0.9 Use caution as you cross paved Elfendahl Pass Road.

1.3 The trail crosses a narrow dirt road.

2.1 Go left on a dirt road for 50 feet then find the trail again on the right.

3.1 Cross South Spillman Road (310 feet).

3.3 The trail crosses another dirt road.

4.2 "T" intersection and a large trail map will help you locate yourself in this rolling forest country. When you are ready to leave go right and head north up the Tahuya River valley.

5.1 An unsigned trail joins the Tahuya River Trail from the right. Continue straight ahead.

5.7 At the edge of the Tahuya River Horse Camp the trail goes right, climbing to a bench.

5.8 Cross the campground access road at the center of a switchback and head back into the forest.

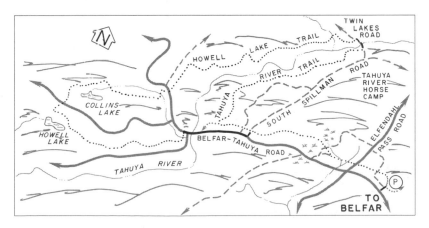

Howell Lake ORV Trail

6.1 Stay to the left at an unmarked "Y" junction.

6.5 At Twin Lakes Road, go left on the road and cross the Tahuya River, then climb past a large gravel pit to find the well-signed Howell Lake Trail on the left (310 feet).

6.6 Go left on the Howell Lake Trail. Under a dense forest cover the trail rolls in and out of narrow creek gullies. This trail is signed with diamond markers and arrows at most intersections.

7.0 The trail divides; stay right.

7.1 Another unmarked intersection. Go left and descend to cross a small creek on a good bridge, then take a sharp left.

7.6 At this and the next two intersections follow the more used-looking trails.

9.3 Head across a giant clearcut. The trail is well signed as it weaves among the logging spurs.

10.0 Intersection; go right on the Howell Lake Loop Trail.

10.1 The trail crosses Bennettsen Lake Road.

10.2 Cycle straight across paved Belfair–Tahuya Road.

11.8 In the midst of a logging clearing, the trail joins an old road.

Go left and watch for views of the Olympics to the west. At the far end of the logging clearing take a right.

12.6 Cross another paved road.

13.1 Cross the dirt road access to Howell Lake Campground (410 feet). This is a good place for a rest stop. To reach the shore of this popular fishing lake, cycle down into the picnic and boat-launch areas. There are no views of the lake from the trail.

13.4 A 5-way intersection. Take the second trail on the right and circle a marsh (not the place to linger in mosquito or duck season), then head back into forest.

15.9 When the loop trail crosses paved Belfair–Tahuya Road, leave the trail and go right on the pavement. Descend to cross the Tahuya River bridge, and pedal up the hill on the other side.

16.9 Go left on gravel-surfaced South Spillman Road.

17.0 Take a right onto the Tahuya River Trail and follow your tracks back to the Mission Creek Trailhead.

20.1 The end of the ride. Give your bike a good massage; it deserves it.

KITSAP PENINSULA

3. Overland to Kamenga Canyon

Loop trip: 11.0 miles
Elevation gain: 600 feet
Map: Tahuya State Forest Map
Best: all year
Allow: 3–4 hours

Description: ORV trail (loose rock and roots, very steep sections); paved road (no shoulders)
Rating: skilled
Info: DNR (South Puget Sound)

Despite the inherent serenity of the beautiful countryside with its peaceful forest, quiet ravines, verdant canyons, and hidden lakes, this trail should be tackled only by riders looking for an adrenaline rush. The Overland Trail to Kamenga Canyon twists and turns like a snake through this scenic section of the Tahuya State Forest. The trail charges straight up and over the low ridges that characterize this area then drops like a lead ball down the opposite side. Wheels spin out in the loose gravel and rocks, and roots will send you flying if you let your attention wander.

Access: Drive Highway 3 to the town of Belfair, then head west on NE Clifton Lane, following the Belfair State Park signs. After

0.1 mile turn right on Old Belfair Highway and follow it north for 3.4 miles before making a left turn on Bear Creek–Dewatto Road. After 3.2 miles the road divides; stay left and continue toward Dewatto for another 2.3 miles. Turn left at Elfendahl Pass Road and park at the Toonerville Campground and Picnic Area (350 feet).

MILEAGE LOG

0.0 From the parking area ride across Bear Creek–Dewatto Road to reach the trailhead. After 50 feet the trail divides, go right towards Kamenga Canyon.

0.9 Cross Bear Creek–Dewatto Road and head south on a trail that is criss-crossed with roads and spur trails.

1.0 The trail is bisected by a road; continue straight ahead.

1.2 Intersection; go right.

1.4 Reach a confusing intersection; go left, paralleling a swampy lake.

1.6 The trail divides; head left, away from the lake. In 300 feet there is another intersection; stay right.

1.7 A secondary trail joins the Overland from the left. Continue straight.

1.8 The trail divides; stay to the right.

2.5 The trail passes the south end of the lake then descends to a bridge.

2.9 A spur trail branches off on the left. Continue straight ahead.

3.3 At the south end of a second shallow lake a road branches off on the right. Continue on the trail.

3.5 The trail ends temporarily. Go right for 15 feet to a road, then head left for 250 feet to find the trail again on the right.

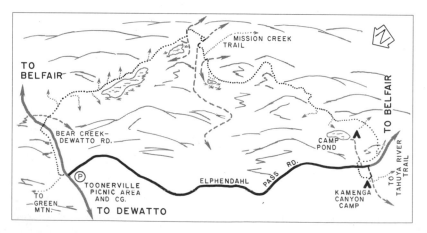

Swampy Lake on the Kamenga Canyon Trail

3.8 The trail divides again. Take your choice; either fork will do. In 200 feet both trails end at a road. Go right for 100 feet then take a left back on the trail.

4.1 A 4-way intersection. To the left is the Mission Creek Trail. Continue straight ahead on the unsigned Overland Trail.

4.2 Go left on a logging road for 75 feet then right, back onto the trail.

4.4 The trail divides again. The right fork descends to the shores of a swamp then rejoins the main trail in 0.2 mile.

5.3 Stay left at this unmarked intersection and at the three following junctions. The trail winds through the forest then descends to the floor of the Tahuya River valley in the Kamenga Canyon area. Numerous spur roads and trails are passed in this section; the main trail is well marked and usually very obvious.

6.9 Intersection; go right, still following the Overland Trail. The valley bottom is nearly level and the trail winds through the trees, crossing a road and unmarked trails. Stay on the widest and most used-looking trail.

7.3 Cross paved Elfendahl Pass Road.

7.6 At Kamenga Canyon Campground go right and follow the road down to the camp area at the edge of the Tahuya River. This is a great place to take a break while you decide whether you would like to turn around and ride the Overland Trail back to the start or complete the loop with a cruise on a paved road. To continue the loop, head up the camp access road.

7.7 Go left on an unsigned forest road.

7.9 Head north (left) on the nearly level Elfendahl Pass Road and ride pavement back to the start.

11.0 The loop ends at the Toonerville Campground and Picnic Area.

KITSAP PENINSULA

4. Not So Bald Point Vista

Round trip: 10.8 miles
Elevation gain: 160 feet
Map: Metsker: Mason County
Best: all year
Allow: 2–3 hours

Description: road; well maintained
Rating: easy
Info: DNR (Enumclaw)

How many middle-aged men do you know who wouldn't give up a 1965 Corvette to learn Bald Point's secrets? Only a few years ago, Bald Point was truly bald. The view from this bald point was so outstanding that the Department of Natural Resources built a picnic area at the very end of the point overlooking The Great Bend of Hood Canal. Today the vegetation has grown back and, while the point still bears the name of Bald, it is anything but.

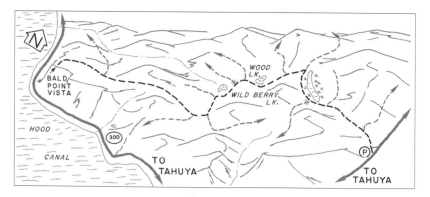

Snooze at the end of the cruise

Despite the diminished view, the ride to Bald Point Vista is worth the effort. The route follows logging roads which wander through clearcuts and tree plantations and past three large lakes. This area is exceptionally beautiful in late May and early June, when the native rhododendrons are in bloom.

Access: Drive to Belfair on Highway 3, then turn west, following the Belfair State Park signs along Highway 300. The state park is passed in 3 miles. Check your odometer and continue west for 11.4 miles along the east side of Hood Canal. Drive across the Tahuya River bridge, then take the first right on NE Belfair–Tahuya Road. In 0.5 mile the road divides; stay left for 1 mile, then go left again on a narrow, unsigned road. Park alongside the road at the turnoff (elevation 350 feet).

MILEAGE LOG

0.0 The ride starts with a descent through a tree farm with excellent views of the Olympic Range.

0.1 Intersection; go left. Some intersections are signed and others are not. To save time and confusion, all major intersections are noted in this log.

0.2 The road divides; stay left.

0.4 Pass a spur road on the right. Continue straight ahead, following the road around the south side of a long, marshy lake.

0.7 Pass a gated road on the left.

1.2 The road divides again. Before following the left fork, look east for a view of Mt. Rainier.

1.6 Stay left at a "Y."

2.2 Look for Wood Lake on the right (380 feet).

2.3 The road divides again; stay left.

2.5 Pass a gated road on the right, then descend briefly to pass Wild Berry Lake (400 feet).

2.8 The road divides; stay left and pedal over the top of a clearcut.

3.1 The road divides; go right. In 20 feet pass a well-marked spur road on the left. Continue straight.

5.2 The road divides; stay left for the final climb to the vista point.

5.4 Bald Point Vista (400 feet). Even though the trees have blocked out much of the view, you can still see two national parks (Mt. Rainier and Olympic), Hood Canal (before and after The Great Bend), the Tacoma City Light powerhouse, the town of Potlatch, and Highway 101.

KITSAP PENINSULA

5. Hahobas Adventure

Round trip: 20.2 miles
Elevation gain: 800 feet
Map: Metsker: Mason County
Best: all year
Allow: 4–5 hours

Description: road (maintained with some very steep sections)
Rating: moderate
Info: none

Riding at the southern end of the Kitsap Peninsula is always an adventure. No map shows all the maintained roads, abandoned logging roads, and jeep roads that wind through this area. Intersections are rarely signed and logging roads are not numbered. Traffic volume is usually light here, making the area perfect for cycling.

This ride is only a sampling of the adventures the Kitsap Peninsula offers. Explorers can spend days on the unmarked maze of roads around Aldrich Lake, riding to hidden lakes, unexpected vistas, and secluded picnic sites along forgotten creeks.

The Hahobas Adventure takes you along the east side of Hood Canal on some of the few roads in this area that are actually signed. The ride begins at Musqueti Point and heads north to the small community of Dewatto. After a short side trip to visit the waterfront the route heads uphill, then inland, to end at the small Aldrich Lake campground.

Access: Drive to the town of Belfair on Highway 3, then, following the Belfair State Park signs, turn west on NE Clifton Lane. In 0.1 mile reach an intersection and continue straight ahead on Highway 300. After 3 miles, pass Belfair State Park. Fill up your water bottles, buy all your last-minute snacks at the park, then check your odometer and continue west along Hood Canal for 15.7 miles to the community of Musqueti Point. (If you cross Rendstand Creek you have gone too far.) Park on the left-hand side of the road in a gravel lot signed "Menard's Landing–Port of Tahuya" (elevation 10 feet).

Blue heron

MILEAGE LOG

0.0 From Menard's Landing, cycle north on the main road paralleling Hood Canal. After a few hundred feet of easy riding the road begins a series of brisk climbs interspersed with steep descents. This sets the pattern for the next 7.6 miles as the road parallels the east bank of the canal. You may catch an occasional view to the west through the dense foliage; however, for most of the distance the road tunnels through forest. To the left you will glimpse an occasional house below the road, and to the right a thin band of trees

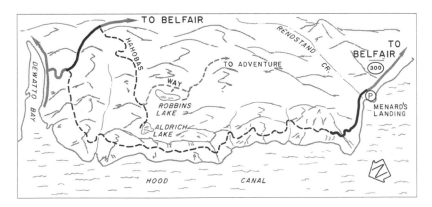

Views extend across the Hood Canal to the Olympic Mountains

hides massive clearcuts on the hillsides above. As private cabins and homes are tucked in small bays along the canal's edge, expect to encounter some traffic.

1.5 Pavement ends. Continue north on a well-maintained dirt road.

7.6 The road ends (220 feet). Go right, uphill, on paved Dewatto Road. **SIDE TRIP:** From the intersection descend 0.5 mile to Dewatto Bay. The bay is peaceful, secluded, and surrounded by private property signs, so you must enjoy the view and a snack from the edge of the road.

8.5 Reach the top of a hill, descend 200 feet, then go right on Hahobas Way (a gravel-covered road).

9.2 The road divides; go right, following the sign to Aldrich Lake. **SIDE TRIP:** From the intersection go left toward Robbins Lake. In 0.8 mile, at the base of a short descent find a well-used, unmarked spur road on the right leading to picnic tables on the shores of Robbins Lake. If you are looking for adventure, continue on past Robbins Lake and explore the new roads and old, abandoned tracks through the clearcuts and tree farms.

9.9 The road divides again; go right, following the signs to Aldrich Lake, and descend to the Department of Natural Resources campground and picnic area.

10.1 The road ends at the west side of Aldrich Lake. Continue on a trail for another 100 feet to a vista point. At one time there was an excellent view from here over Hood Canal to Mt. Ellinor and Mt. Washington, the Skokomish River valley, and the town of Lilliwaup. The viewpoint is now overgrown and only very tall cyclists will be able to see the tips of the mountains over the tree tops.

Before heading back, look for the still-visible signs of old logging operations in the area. Aldrich Lake was used in the early 1900s as a log dump. From the lake the logs were sent over the hill, down a flume, for the long plunge into Hood Canal. A deep gully, site of the old flume, can still be found on the steep hillside.

When you are ready, retrace the route back to Menard's Landing.

ISSAQUAH

6. Tiger Mountain by Road

Summit Loop
Round trip: 20.3 miles
Elevation gain: 2,804 feet
Map: DNR: Tiger Mountain
Best: March–November
Allow: 2–3 hours
Description: road; one rough section
Rating: moderate
Info: DNR (Enumclaw)

Short Loop
Round Trip: 12.1 miles
Elevation gain: 1,939 feet
Map: DNR: Tiger Mountain
Best: March–November
Allow: 2–3 hours
Description: road; one rough section
Rating: moderate
Info: DNR (Enumclaw)

Tiger Mountain is actually a group of five hills, the highest being East Tiger Mountain, the lowest being West Tiger No. 3. It's a popular place—which means Tiger Mountain is not the place to ride if you're looking for a quiet forest retreat. With easy access from around Puget Sound, the roads here attract mountain bikers, horse riders, motorcyclists, and the occasional family group out for a walk. On the upper reaches of the mountain you will meet hikers, bird watchers, and joggers, who have their own routes to the summit. You may also encounter loggers and maintenance crews for the relay towers decorating the summits.

If you don't mind the commotion, you'll discover excellent riding on Tiger Mountain. Narrow forest roads offer a good workout while climbing to scenic overlooks and a fast-paced thrill while descending.

Two routes are suggested here: the Summit Loop Ride, which encompasses two of the summits, and the Short Loop, which takes in only East Tiger Mountain. If you enjoy view gazing, pack a large lunch and spend time at each summit.

Access: Drive 8 miles east of Issaquah on Interstate 90 to Exit 25. Head south 4.2 miles on Highway 18 to a large parking area at the summit of the pass (1,377 feet).

SUMMIT LOOP MILEAGE LOG

0.0 Two roads start from the parking lot. Follow gated Tiger Mountain Road, which heads north (right) for 0.1 mile.

0.1 At the first corner look for an open space on the right. Head into the forest, then go left for 100 feet, then right on a well-used trail. Wind through the trees for 300 yards to a large powerline clearing. Turn left again and head north, climbing then descending the powerline road. This road is rough, steep, and difficult to negotiate in sections. The road divides several times; pick whichever branch looks easiest, as the roads will rejoin farther along.

Don't get discouraged, this is the most difficult section of the loop ride.

1.2 The powerline road reaches East Side Road (1,120 feet). Go left on this well-maintained logging road and enjoy views of Rattlesnake Mountain and the Snoqualmie Valley.

1.6 Pass the Northwest Timber Trail on left (see Route 7).

2.4 The road enters the forest, descends to Trout Hatchery Creek, and climbs to an old railroad grade.

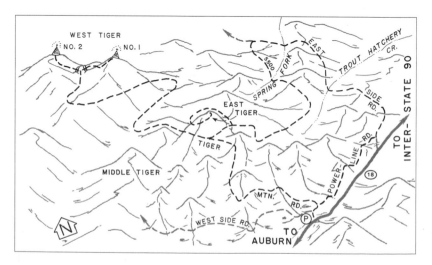

2.6 Pass an unmarked spur road heading left.

4.4 Intersection; go left on Road 5500 (1,468 feet). This road climbs steadily through evergreen and deciduous forest, becoming steeper as you near the summit.

4.5 Pass the Preston Railroad Grade Trail access on right.

7.1 Ridge crest and viewpoint (2,670 feet).

7.2 Intersection. Take the upper (right-hand) road and head up the final pitch to East Tiger Mountain.

8.0 East Tiger Mountain summit (3,004 feet). Here you can enjoy views of Maple Valley, McDonald and Grass Mountains, the Three Sisters, Carbon Ridge, and Mt. Rainier to the south. Trees block the rest of the views and one can't help wishing that the old fire lookout, which stood on a 90-foot tower, still existed.

Once you have taken in the view, descend back to the main road.

8.8 Back at the intersection, go right and descend the south side of East Tiger Mountain.

9.3 Intersection (2,400 feet). Go right (up) on Tiger Mountain Road. (Short Loop riders will go left here and descend back to

Cyclists descending from West Tiger Mountain

the parking lot. Summit Loop riders will return to this point on the way back and follow the left fork to the parking lot.)

9.8 Pass the upper end of the Preston Railroad Grade Trail then pedal over a low, forested saddle, before descending.

11.2 The descent ends (2,080 feet). The road now heads east, climbing gradually, with occasional viewpoints north and east.

13.4 The road divides. Go right and ride or push your bike 0.1 mile up to the summit of West Tiger No. 1 (2,948 feet). When ready, head back down the steep road.

17.5 Stay right at East Tiger Mountain Road and continue the descent.

20.3 The parking lot marks the end of the loop.

SHORT LOOP MILEAGE LOG

0.0 Follow the Summit Loop Log for 9.3 miles.

9.3 Go left and descend on Tiger Mountain Road.

12.1 The loop ends at the parking lot.

ISSAQUAH

7. Tiger Mountain by Trail

Loop trip: 11.2 miles
Elevation gain: 1,123 feet
Map: DNR: Tiger Mountain
Best: May 15–October 15
Allow: 2–3 hours

Description: road (well maintained); trail (very rough)
Rating: skilled
Info: DNR (Enumclaw)

Forest scenes rather than grand vistas provide the visual stimulation on this very challenging road and trail loop. The road part is easy, with well-graded, well-maintained roads connecting the two trails. The two trails on this loop differ radically in quality. The Preston Railroad Grade is a primitive trail that crosses endless exposed tree roots and, for most of the year, giant mud holes. The Northwest Timber Trail is beautifully constructed, and riding is nearly effortless on its smooth tread.

Please keep in mind that both the trails and roads have multiple-use designations. Watch for hikers and horse riders. Be courteous and friendly and get out of the way of all other users. Not only is it the polite thing to do, but it is the only way mountain bikers can count on continued use of these excellent single-track trails.

Don't expect to have the trail all to yourself.

Please note that this trail is open from May 15 to October 15 only.

Access: Drive I-90 east from Issaquah for 8 miles to Exit 25. Head south on Highway 18 for 4.2 miles to the Tiger Mountain Summit (that is the road summit only). Park in the large dirt lot on the right-hand (west) side of the road (1,377 feet).

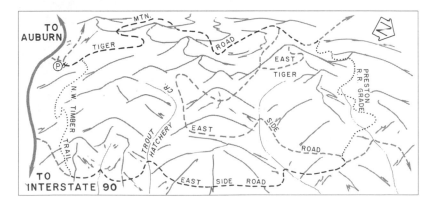

MILEAGE LOG

0.0 Two roads take off at the northern end of the parking lot. Your loop follows Tiger Mountain Road on the right. Cycle around the gate then head north, climbing steadily.

0.2 Pass the Northwest Timber Trail on the right. For now stay on the road; you will return to this point by the trail.

2.8 East Tiger Mountain Road branches off to the right. Continue straight, climbing steadily.

3.2 Leave the road and go right on the Preston Railroad Grade Trail. The trail starts off with an initial climb then settles into a rolling traverse of the forested hillside.

4.0 The trail follows the route of the old railroad grade.

6.7 The Preston Railroad Grade Trail ends with a fun descent to the road. Go right and descend to a 3-way intersection.

6.8 A 3-way intersection. Head to the right on East Side Road (1,468 feet). This well-graded road descends to Trout Hatchery Creek then climbs.

8.7 Leave the road and head uphill to the right on the well-graded Northwest Timber Trail. This is a wide, easy-riding trail that climbs gradually through an old clearcut then heads into the forest. Along the way you will encounter a couple of very tight switchbacks and two very solid bridges.

11.0 The trail ends at Tiger Mountain Road. Go left and descend.

11.2 The parking lot and end of the ride.

When we grow up we're going to be fully suspended.

View over the Puget Sound Basin from Rattlesnake Mountain

8. Rattlesnake Mountain

Loop trip: 15.7 miles
Elevation gain: 2,400 feet
Maps: USGS: North Bend, Hobart, and Fall City
Best: March–October

Allow: 4–5 hours
Description: road; steep and rough in sections
Rating: moderate
Info: none

Rattlesnake Mountain is a long ridge overlooking the South Fork Snoqualmie River Valley, Interstate 90, North Bend, and the Cascade Mountains on the east and the Issaquah Alps and Puget Sound basin on the west. Although the hillsides have been stripped of their forests and the ridge crest dotted with telephone and radio relay towers, the riding is outstanding.

The loop climbs over the summit ridge of Rattlesnake Mountain then descends along the Raging River drainage. The ride is

51

entirely on logging roads, some in excellent condition, some steep and rough. The road is gated at the base so the entire ride may be vehicle-free when loggers aren't working the area.

Access: Drive Interstate 90 east from Issaquah for 8 miles to Exit 25. Turn south on Highway 18 for 0.1 mile, then take the first left on SE 104th Street. Go straight for 200 feet then park in the large open area at the right-hand side of the road (elevation 900 feet).

MILEAGE LOG

0.0 Head out on the dirt road that begins at the southeast corner of the parking area. Cycle past the gate, then over Lake Creek (a large marsh). The road surface is hard-packed gravel, very easy to ride on. Several spur roads branch off; however, the main road is obvious and well marked with "35000" or "MLRS" signs.

 The road climbs easily as it heads southeast up the broad Raging River Valley. Clearcuts and powerline cuts have opened views to Brew Hill, Taylor Mountain, and Tiger Mountain.

0.9 The road divides at a power substation. Stay left and pass a gate, climbing gradually on the 35000 Road. There is one short and very steep climb on this section, which begins after the road crosses Canyon Creek at 2.5 miles. At the top there is a view of Mt. Rainier.

3.4 Stay right at a junction, still following the 35000 Road.

4.0 Unmarked intersection; stay left.

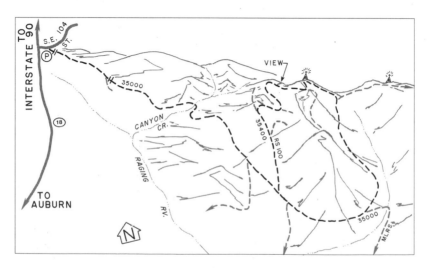

Early winter snow adds extra interest to the descent.

4.4 Turn left on a road signed as number 35400 and RS 100 (1,834 feet). This road is steep and rough, climbing through forest plantations to the summit.

5.2 Unmarked intersection; stay left.

6.4 The road divides; stay right.

6.6 The road divides again; stay right.

6.8 Major intersection; continue straight ahead.

7.3 An unmarked spur road on the left leads to an awesome view over the South Fork Snoqualmie River to North Bend, the city of Snoqualmie, Mt. Si, Mt. Teneriffe, Grouse Ridge,

Bandera Mountain, Mt. Washington, and north over the Weyerhaeuser Snoqualmie Tree Farm.

7.9 On a broad landing directly below the relay tower, the road divides. Pause to soak in the view over Lake Sammamish, Lake Washington, and Puget Sound before taking the road on the left (35500 Road) for the final climb to the relay towers and the forested ridgetop.

8.1 The climb ends at 3,262 feet. This is not the highest summit of Rattlesnake Mountain; however, let it suffice for this ride. (The highest summit, 3,517 feet, lies at the edge of the Cedar River Watershed. So rather than be tempted by miles of forbidden roads, descend here.)

8.5 Pass the road to the highest summit on the left. Stay to the right and continue to descend.

10.0 Intersection. Go right, once again on the 35000 Road (MLRS) (2,170 feet).

11.3 Pass the 35400 Road to close the loop portion of the ride. Retrace your route down the 35000 Road.

15.7 The loop ends at SE 104th Street.

SNOQUALMIE PASS

9. Iron Horse 1—Snoqualmie Pass Tunnel Ride

Round Trip

Round trip: 35.2 miles
Elevation gain: 1,620 feet
Map: USFS: North Bend RD
Best: mid-June–mid-October
Allow: 5–6 hours
Description: railroad grade with a short steep section
Rating: easy
Info: Lake Easton State Park

One Way

One way: 17.6 miles
Elevation loss: 1,620 feet
Map: USFS: North Bend RD
Best: mid-June–mid-October
Allow: 1–2 hours
Description: railroad grade with a short steep section
Rating: easy
Info: Lake Easton State Park

It's dark, it's dank, it's spooky . . . it's the 2.3-mile-long Snoqualmie Pass Tunnel and in its darkest reaches you will come to the high point of this fascinating ride *through* Snoqualmie Pass.

It may seem odd, with a tunnel as the principal attraction, to talk about scenery, but this ride is wonderfully scenic. The old Milwaukee Railroad grade, now Iron Horse State Park, makes its

The tunnel is really dark.

gradual climb to Snoqualmie Pass along steep hillsides high above Interstate 90. With the valley below and the rugged peaks above, you will not lack for things to look at.

This is a long ride, and it is worth every turn of the pedal. However, if the distance seems a bit daunting, arrange a one-way ride from the pass down. The two-car shuttle takes a little time to

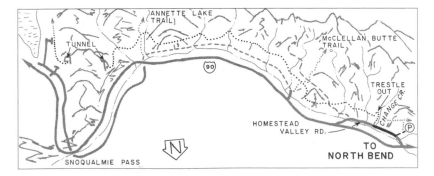

arrange but the 17.6-mile ride down from the pass is certifiably sweat-free.

This ride requires that you add a few extra pieces of gear to your regular kit. Be sure and have a good light with fresh batteries for the tunnel. A bike light or a headlamp that will attach to your helmet is best. Pack a warm jacket; it is very cold in the tunnel. You may also want to add a rain jacket, to protect yourself from the constant drips.

Access: Drive east from North Bend on Interstate 90 to Exit 38 (signed to the Fire Training Academy). Go right on Homestead Valley Road for 0.1 mile then turn right again on a gravel road. Pass a gate, which should be open, and head up for 0.1 mile to the parking area (1,280 feet). If you are doing a One-Way ride, leave one car at this point then drive on up Homestead Valley Road to rejoin Interstate 90. Continue on up and over Snoqualmie Pass then follow the directions given in Route 10 to the Keechelus Lake Trailhead of the Iron Horse State Park.

ONE-WAY MILEAGE LOG

Start your trip at the 17.6-mile point of the Round-Trip Mileage Log. Your mileages will be found in parentheses after the Round-Trip mileages.

ROUND-TRIP MILEAGE LOG

0.0 From the parking area, ride back down to paved Homestead Valley Road.

0.1 Go right and head up Homestead Valley Road.

1.0 As the road crosses Change Creek, look up to see the broken trestle above. About 50 feet after crossing the creek, find a white gate and an old road on the right. Head up and begin the most difficult section of this otherwise easy ride. Stay with the rough road, avoiding all spurs on the left as it climbs to the base of the trestle.

1.2 Go beyond the base of the trestle. As the road peters out, look for a trail on the left and head up, either pushing or carrying your bike to the railroad grade.

1.3 You made the grade—the rest is easy. Go left and head up the valley.

2.3 Cross a trestle, intact, over Hall Creek.

3.2 Ride around a gate. After crossing a road and a parking area, ride around a second gate and back onto the railroad grade.

5.2 The McClellan Butte Trail (closed to mountain bikes) crosses the railroad grade at Alice Creek.

10.4 Hansen Creek and road are crossed on a curved trestle.

East entrance to the tunnel

12.4 The trail goes around an abandoned snowshed.

12.8 The Annette Lake Trail (closed to mountain bikes) crosses the railroad grade.

13.8 Cross Olallie Creek; your feet may get wet here in the early summer.

14.5 Tunnel entrance. Strap on your headlamp and don your warm clothes before heading in. Use caution and watch for other users in the dark tunnel.

16.8 Exit the tunnel.

17.0 Pass a gate and continue straight through the residential area below Hyak Ski Resort.

17.6 **(0.0)** The Keechelus Lake Trailhead of the Iron Horse State Park is located on the left. This is a good turnaround point. Restroom facilities are available.

18.4 **(0.8)** Turn your lights back on and head back through the tunnel. In this direction you will be able to see the light at the end of the tunnel for most of the ride. Try not to look at the bright daylight while you are riding or you will lose your night vision.

20.7 **(3.1)** Exit the tunnel and head downvalley.

22.8 **(5.2)** Pass the closed snowshed.

24.8 **(7.2)** Hansen Creek is crossed on curved trestle.

31.9 (14.3) Pass a gate, cross a road, then ride around a second gate.

32.8 (15.2) Cross a trestle.

33.7 (16.1) Pass a small "Bridge Out" sign which is partially hidden in the bushes on the left.

33.9 (16.3) Arrive at the broken trestle. Stop here, do not proceed. NO gate marks the end of the trestle and it is a long way to the bottom. Just before the trestle, look for a well-used trail on the left. Most people will prefer to walk their bikes down the steep grade.

34.0 (16.4) At the base of the old trestle, follow an old road down the hillside.

34.2 (16.6) Go left on the paved road.

35.1 (17.5) Take a left turn on a dirt road and ride up to the parking area.

35.2 (17.6) Ride ends at the parking lot.

SNOQUALMIE PASS

10. Keechelus Lake Loop

Loop trip: 20.3 miles
Elevation gain: 900 feet
Map: Green Trails: Snoqualmie Pass
Best: mid-June–mid-October

Allow: 3–4 hours
Description: road (well maintained); railroad grade
Rating: easy
Info: Cle Elum RS

This may come as a quiet surprise, but the ride loop around Keechelus Lake is actually very scenic. Along this route you'll find excellent viewpoints of Rampart and Box Ridges, the Snoqualmie Pass complex, and Keechelus Lake.

In order to loop around the lake, you will ride logging roads, paved roads, and the old railroad grade. On most of the roads, traffic volume is light. On the railroad grade, which is reserved for nonmotorized recreation, your only concerns will be hikers, horses, and other cyclists (a combination that is potentially more dangerous than logging trucks).

Access: On the east side of Snoqualmie Pass, take Exit 54 off Interstate 90 and drive towards the Hyak Ski Area. Just before the entrance to the large Hyak parking lot, turn left on a road that parallels Interstate 90. After 0.4 mile turn right on a road signed to Iron Horse State Park. Follow this road for 0.7 mile to the Keechelus Lake Trailhead. Park here (2,560 feet).

MILEAGE LOG

0.0 Head back the way you came, following the paved access road for 0.7 mile.

0.7 Turn left, paralleling the very noisy interstate.

1.1 The road ends; go right and ride under the freeway and through the freeway interchange area to the Gold Creek Sno-Park.

1.4 Take a left turn on the paved Gold Creek Road and follow it down the valley. This peaceful 2-lane road is the old U.S. Highway 10, once the main route over Snoqualmie Pass. The road is too close to the noise and grime of Interstate 90 to be considered enjoyable; however, traffic is light and the view up the Gold Creek valley is beautiful.

3.7 Pavement ends and the road begins to climb with steep switchbacks up the side of Keechelus Ridge. The road name changes from Gold Creek Road to Road 4832. Once you work your way above the initial band of trees, look behind you for views over Interstate 90, the Snoqualmie Pass ski resorts, and Bryant Peak.

5.3 The road divides; go right, still on Road 4832.

5.5 Resort Creek Pond, complete with lilies and frogs, lies just off the road to the left. At 3,380 feet, this is the highest point of the loop and a great place for a rest stop. Beyond the lake the road crosses a low saddle then heads down. Watch for a view of Keechelus Lake and the Yakima River Valley at a sharp corner.

7.3 Shortly after crossing Resort Creek the descent ends and the road begins a rolling traverse along the flanks of Kachess Ridge. Traffic volume is usually low as you alternate from

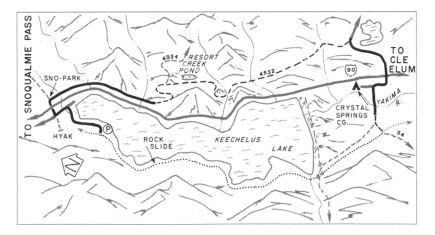

Overview of Keechelus Lake and Mt. Rainier

clearcut to young forest. There are some private residences in this area.

10.8 Road 4832 ends. Go right on the paved and often busy Lake Kachess Road.

11.6 Cross the freeway on a overpass then continue straight ahead on paved Crystal Springs/Stampede Pass Road.

12.1 Pass the entrance to Crystal Springs Campground. Running water, toilets, and picnic tables are available there; however, the constant roar from Interstate 90 is intrusive and anyone making a prolonged stop will soon find themselves wishing that they had lost their hearing at a rock concert twenty years ago.

12.2 Cross the Yakima River.

12.8 Intersection and end of the pavement. Go straight ahead on Road 54.

13.0 When the road crosses the railroad grade, turn right and head west following the route of the old Milwaukee Railroad grade, which is now part of Iron Horse State Park (2,480 feet).

14.5 A gate serves warning of an upcoming road crossing. Shortly beyond you will cross the first of several bridges. Gravel on the bridges is deep and soft so hold on tight to the handle bars and pedal fast.

18.1 The railroad grade enters a rock slide area. Unfortunately, this is also one of the best viewpoints along the lake. Look at the view as you ride, but do not linger.

20.3 The loop ends when the railroad grade reaches the Keechelus Lake Trailhead.

SNOQUALMIE PASS

11. Amabilis Mountain Loop

Round trip: 10.6 miles
Elevation gain: 2,094 feet
Map: Green Trails: Snoqualmie Pass
Best: June–mid-October

Allow: 3–4 hours
Description: road; well maintained
Rating: moderate
Info: Cle Elum RS

Amabilis Mountain is a must for all view-loving mountain bikers. Views start early and expand to panoramic proportions at the summit. To name a few highlights: you will look down on both Keechelus and Kachess Lakes, southwest to Mt. Rainier, north to Rampart and Chikamin Ridges, east to French Cabin Mountain, and west to Stampede Pass.

The loop is almost entirely on well-maintained logging roads. The climb up is steady and the descent steep enough to be fast and fun. Traffic is light, except when the loggers are skinning off

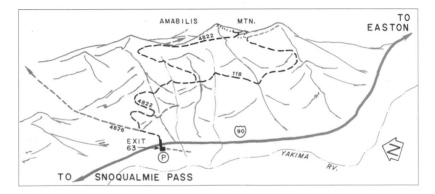

Cyclist near the summit of Amabilis Mountain

another section of the forest. On weekends, however, expect to see numerous view seekers, firewood gatherers, hunters, and huckleberry pickers in all types of vehicles.

Access: Drive Interstate 90 east 11.5 miles from Snoqualmie Pass to Exit 63, signed "Cabin Creek." Turn west and park in the large winter Sno-Park parking area (2,460 feet).

MILEAGE LOG

0.0 From the Sno-Park, cycle over Interstate 90 and straight onto Road 4826.

0.3 Go right on Road 4822 and begin the climb up Amabilis Mountain. Several spur roads are passed on the climb; stay on the obvious main road.

2.7 The road divides (at 3,400 feet), marking the start of the actual loop portion of the ride. Go right on Spur Road 118 and head up one long switchback to the summit.

5.0 At 4,500 feet the road crosses over the top of a clearcut, then turns sharply right and reenters the forest. At the start of the turn, find a rough jeep road on the left and follow it across the clearcut hillside.

5.1 The jeep road divides; stay to the right and ride towards the ridge crest.

5.2 The jeep road reaches an established logging road and ends. Go left and follow the road over the ridge crest, heading west.

5.3 The road divides. To descend, go straight on Road 4822. *SIDE TRIP:* Before starting down, check out the views from the ridgetop. Take the road on the right and head up the gradual slope for 100 yards then head right on a short, unsigned spur road. After 50 feet go left on an old cat road and follow it up a rock rib which sticks up above the rest of the ridge crest (4,554 feet). Scramble to the top of the rocks and spend some time sunbathing and enjoying the view.

7.9 Road 4822 and Spur Road 118 rejoin, closing the loop section of the ride.

10.6 Done already? You shouldn't have ridden so fast.

12. Iron Horse 2 — Easton to Cle Elum

One way: 11.5 miles
Elevation loss: 640 feet
Map: USFS: Cle Elum RD
Best: May–October
Allow: 2–3 hours

Description: Railroad grade; graveled
Rating: easy
Info: Lake Easton State Park

Once a major railroad link across the state, the old Milwaukee Road is now an important cornerstone in the Rails-to-Trails program in Washington State. The old railroad bed, minus the tracks where the electric-powered trains rattled and rumbled, is an ideal mountain bike ride. Riders who rattle and rumble along this long corridor are free from the worry of mechanized vehicles and can relax and enjoy wildlife viewing, a scenic look at the upper Yakima River valley, a quiet picnic, or just good old exercise.

The old railroad grade is part of Iron Horse State Park. The park extends from North Bend all the way east to Vantage on the Columbia River. Unfortunately, people who thought they could have free land after the railroad left are disputing the right-of-way and a couple of key sections are still closed to the public; of particular importance is the section between Stampede Pass Road and the town of Easton.

This ride was designed as an easy one-way trip from Easton to South Cle Elum; however, if you are looking for a good workout, do a round trip. Riding the railroad grade is easy, and 23 miles will speed past, leaving time for a side trip to Cle Elum for ice cream before heading back.

Home with a view

Access: Drive Interstate 90 east from Snoqualmie Pass and take Exit 71 at the town of Easton. Go right and head straight across town. Cross the main street and drive up a short hill to the intersection of Cabin Creek Road and 2nd Street. Leave the pavement and go left, on well-graveled road along the crest of the railroad grade. After 0.2 mile look for a large parking area on your right.

Your shuttle car should be left at the South Cle Elum Trailhead. See Route 13 for driving instructions.

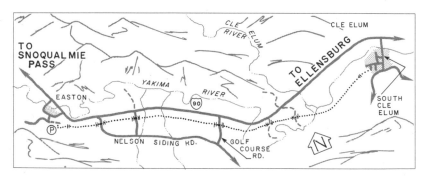

MILEAGE LOG

0.0 From the Easton Trailhead, plant your aluminum, titanium, or chrome-moly steel horse on the railroad grade, point your front wheel east, put your feet on the pedals, and go. Riding difficulty and conditions do not change much from this point on. Spend your time enjoying the mountain air and looking for wildlife. Deer and elk are often seen along the railroad grade while eagles and a variety of feathered friends dot the sky, lakes, trees, and fields. Sound of the freeway will filter through for the next few miles.

2.1 Cross paved Nelson Siding Road.

3.5 An old trestle takes you over Big Creek.

6.2 Cross paved Golf Course Road.

6.9 Ride the old trestle high above the Yakima River.

7.1 Cross a dirt road.

8.3 Another dirt road is crossed.

9.4 Ride over the Yakima River for a second time.

10.7 Cycle around a gate.

11.5 Go left to end the ride at the South Cle Elum Trail Access. If you reach a paved road with a blocked trail ahead you have gone too far and must backtrack 100 feet to find the parking area.

Rider on the Iron Horse Trail

13. Iron Horse 3—South Cle Elum to the Yakima River Gorge

Round trip: 15 miles
Elevation loss: 170 feet
Maps: Green Trails: Cle Elum and Thorp
Best: March–November

Allow: 3–4 hours
Description: railroad grade
Rating: easy
Info: Lake Easton State Park

The Iron Horse Trail is a perfect trip for families, large groups, and beginning mountain bike riders. Without the worry of motorized traffic, you may enjoy the luxury of riding in groups on the wide railroad grade as well as a conversation with your fellow riders.

On this ride of the Iron Horse Trail (see Routes 9, 10, and 12 for more Iron Horse riding) the railroad grade parallels the course of the Yakima River through open farmland to a narrow gorge. Since the river valley gets very hot in the summer, carry plenty of extra water. Do not drink from any of the streams along the way, and watch out for rattlesnakes.

Access: Drive Interstate 90 east from Snoqualmie Pass for 22 miles. Take Exit 84 and drive 0.7 mile toward Cle Elum. As the road descends into town, turn right on Rossette Street, following signs to South Cle Elum. In the next 0.9 mile the road passes under the freeway, crosses the Yakima River, enters South Cle Elum, and becomes Fourth Street. Turn right off Fourth Street at Madison Avenue, following signs to Iron Horse State Park. After 0.2 mile turn left on West Cozy Corner then make an immediate right on 602 Milwaukee Avenue. Drive 0.1 mile to find

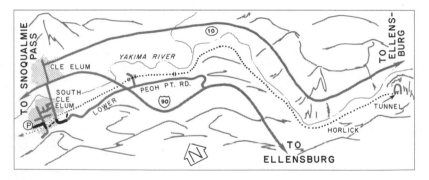

the South Cle Elum Trailhead parking area and toilets on the left (1,920 feet).

MILEAGE LOG

0.0 The Rails-to-Trails concept has met with a great deal of opposition from private landowners, who hope to incorporate the land abandoned by the railroad into their own property free of charge. The state purchased a total of 25 miles of trail from the railroad company, but has been forced to go to court over a succession of illegal fences and blockades put up by land grabbers. The start of this ride is one such area so you must begin your trip with a short ride on the city streets.

From the parking area go right and ride back the way you came on 602 Milwaukee Ave.

0.1 Turn right on West Cozy Corner for 150 feet then go left on a rough gravel road that parallels the railroad grade.

0.3 At the stop sign go right on the paved road then head east on Lower Peoh Point Road.

0.5 Just before Lower Peoh Point Road begins to climb, cross to the left side and find a gravel road. Follow this road along the valley bottom.

0.7 Pass a gate and head east on the old railroad grade. Views are blocked by high walls of brush.

3.2 The railroad grade passes under Interstate 90.

3.4 The trail is intersected by a paved road; look both ways before crossing.

4.5 A gate and a portable toilet mark the beginning of the wilderness portion of this ride. Pedal east past a small farm. On the left lies the Yakima River, heading swiftly eastward

An immature hawk

The Yakima River

to join the Columbia. To the northeast the Stuart Range is visible above the trees.

5.5 The railroad grade leaves the river's edge at the confluence of the Teanaway and Yakima Rivers and tunnels through a grove of trees.

7.9 The grade returns to the edge of the river. Cycle under a broad powerline swath, then enter an isolated section of farmland known as Bristel Flat.

9.8 A couple of old overgrown shacks mark the site of Horlick, a small ghost town. From here on the valley narrows and the railroad grade cuts across steep canyon walls only a few feet above the sweeping torrent of the Yakima River.

12.0 The valley bends, the Yakima River flows through a narrow box canyon, and the railroad grade heads through a tunnel. If you brought your flashlight, it is fun to explore the old tunnel before heading back to South Cle Elum.

After riding this short section of trail, think about how much fun you would have if you could start in Seattle and ride all the way to Spokane. Imagine the adventures along the way as you pedal over mountains, rivers, and plains, camping in quiet country and visiting little towns. This is the dream behind the Rails-to-Trails movement, which would convert the abandoned railway lines around the state into a network of trails.

If you would like to learn more about this effort, write to the Rails-to-Trails Conservancy, Suite 304, 1701 K Street NW; Washington, DC 20006.

CLE ELUM

14. The Iron Bear

Loop trip: 20.8 miles
Elevation gain: 2,480 feet
Map: Green Trails: Mt. Stuart and Liberty
Best: mid-June–September
Allow: 5–6 hours

Description: road (well maintained); trail (well maintained with some slippery sections)
Rating: Adventurous
Info: Cle Elum RS

People might, mistakenly, conclude that the name of the Iron Bear Trail was derived from the drainages it follows—those of us who have ridden this trail know better. It takes the strength of a bear to keep a firm grip on the brakes and arms of iron to keep the wheels centered on the trail.

Access: Follow Interstate 90 to the east side of Cle Elum to

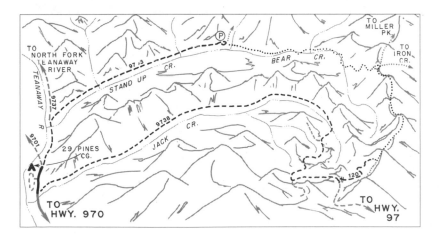

Balsam root blooming on the crest of Teanaway Ridge

Exit 85. Drive 6.2 miles toward Wenatchee on Highway 970, then turn left and follow Teanaway Road then North Fork Teanaway Road for 13.5 miles to the end of the pavement where the road divides. Take the right fork, Road 9737. After 1.4 miles go right on Road 9703 and follow it for 3.4 miles to its end at the Bear Miller Trailhead (3,200 feet).

MILEAGE LOG

0.0 From the parking lot, follow your car's tracks back down-valley. Use these first few easy miles to warm up your legs before starting the long climb up Teanaway Ridge.

0.9 Pass the Stanford Creek Trailhead on the right then roll across Stanford Creek on a solid bridge.

2.7 Pass a road on the right which leads to the Standup Trail. Shortly after, cross the Standup Creek bridge.

3.4 Intersection; go left on Road 9737 and continue down the valley.

4.8 Stay left at a "Y" intersection and continue downvalley on paved North Fork Teanaway Road.

4.9 Pass 29 Pines Campground.

5.1 Turn left on Jack Creek Road No. 9738. At this point you will leave the pavement and begin the long climb out of the valley (2,680 feet). The climb begins gradually as the road heads up through wide grassy meadows. Keep an eye out for stray cows and fast-moving logging trucks.

6.8 The smooth gravel surface gives way to a section of old holey pavement sprinkled with slippery rocks.

8.8 Cross a cattle guard and enter National Forest land. From this point on the climb steepens. Spur roads branch off on both sides of the road as you go. Stay with the obvious main road and continue to climb.

11.8 Ride straight through a major intersection. Watch for an occasional view of Mt. Stuart to the north as you climb.

Teanaway Ridge Trail

12.8 As an extra bonus for the view seeker, Mt. Rainier appears briefly to the southwest. Near this point you will pass two unmarked "Y" intersections. Stay left at the first and right at the second. Shortly after the second intersection the road descends briefly to pass a marshy pond before resuming the ascent.

13.8 Ride across the 4,880-foot crest of Teanaway Ridge. After descending 100 feet head left on gated Spur

Road 120. (This is the second road on the left past the ridge crest.)

14.9 Spur Road 120 ends. Look for the unsigned Teanaway Ridge Trail on the right. This trail ascends for 150 feet then intersects a spur trail. Go left and head up a steep hill.

15.1 At 4,943 feet this knoll is the highest elevation on this loop. Views at this point are limited; better vista points are still ahead. The trail follows the ridge crest, diving and climbing like a hunting falcon.

15.8 Pass the best viewpoint of this ride. Or were you having too much fun to notice?

17.2 Arrive at a 4-way junction. At this point you will leave the Teanaway Ridge Trail and head left, west, down Iron Bear Trail No. 1351. Put on your best bear-sized grin, grip the handle bars, and get ready for a 1,000-foot drop.

17.9 Cross the South Fork of Bear Creek. You will cross it two more times in the next 0.2 mile. In early season this little creek is a refreshing splash; by late summer it is nothing more than a dust bowl.

18.3 Pass a hunters' camp on the right and splash through six creeks in the next 0.5 mile.

19.3 Cross the North Fork of Bear Creek with a big splash.

20.8 Cross Miller Creek before ending your loop at the parking lot. Grrrrrr. Wasn't that fun?

CLE ELUM

15. Teanaway Ridge Ride

Loop trip: 18.0 miles
Elevation gain: 2,143 feet
Map: Green Trails: Liberty
Best: July–October
Allow: 2–3 hours

Description: road (well maintained); ORV trail (narrow, steep, and sandy in sections)
Rating: skilled
Info: Cle Elum RS

The combination of challenging roads, motorcycle trails, and views makes this an exciting loop. The ride starts in the Swauk Creek Valley then climbs to the crest of Teanaway Ridge. From the heights, views of the rolling Wenatchee Mountains, pyramidal Miller Peak, and the needlelike crest of the Stuart Range fill the horizon.

The loop spends a short time on paved highway before starting

Opposite: *Cruising the open country near the crest of Teanaway Ridge*

Indian paintbrush

the climb to the ridge on easy-to-ride logging roads. Once up on Teanaway Ridge, the route follows a trail that looks easy but is treacherously narrow and slippery. The trail broadens for the final descent into Iron Creek, cutting across steep hill-sides in a manner pleasing the claustrophobic but terrorizing the acrophobic. The final stage of the loop is a restful glide down the Iron Creek Valley.

Carry plenty of water; Teanaway Ridge is hot and dusty in summer.

Access: From the intersection of Highways 97 and 970, drive north toward Swauk Pass on Highway 97 for 8.7 miles. Turn left on Iron Creek Road No. 9714, and park well off to the side (2,900 feet).

MILEAGE LOG

0.0 Surprise! Start the loop off by cycling back *down* Highway 97. The shoulder is wide until the Blue Creek bridge.

2.1 Cross Blue Creek, then turn right on Blue Creek Road No. 9738 (2,800 feet), and commence the long uphill grind. Watch for views of Red Top Mountain Lookout ahead.

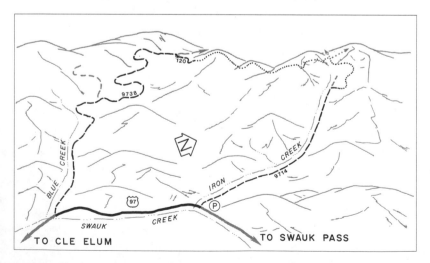

4.8 The road divides; stay right and continue sweating.

8.4 The road arrives at a forested saddle on Teanaway Ridge (4,800 feet) and heads down the other side. A few feet before the ridge crest, turn right on Spur Road 120, ride around the gate, then descend north through clearcuts.

9.5 The road ends in a small turnaround; Teanaway Ridge Trail (unsigned) begins from the far right-hand side of the turnaround. Follow the trail 150 feet up to the ridge crest where you will intersect a second, unsigned trail. Turn left and ride or push north, up the steep trail.

9.7 Highest point on the loop (4,943 feet). The trail continues along the narrow ridge crest, going up and down like a yo-yo.

12.9 Four-way intersection (4,450 feet). Following the Bear–Iron Trail head down to your right and descend into the Iron Creek drainage. The Bear–Iron Trail is easy to ride but watch your speed, or you may go tumbling down the (aieeee!) steep hillside.

14.7 The Bear–Iron Trailhead and parking area (3,600 feet). Go left on Iron Creek Road, cruising easily downhill.

14.9 Intersection; go left. Cross a creek (wet in early summer).

18.0 Iron Creek Road ends at Highway 97 and the car.

CLE ELUM

16. Naneum Rock Garden

Loop trip: 8.9 miles
Elevation gain: 1,000 feet
Maps: Green Trails: Liberty and Thorp
Best: July–September

Allow: 3–4 hours
Description: trails; in bad shape with ruts, rocks, and sand
Rating: adventurous
Info: Cle Elum RS

If you are looking for a true test of your mountain bike skills, Naneum Rock Garden is the place. On rugged ORV trails you will discover whether your riding has taken you into the next dimension (beyond the limits of space, time, and gravity) or if you still need to work on your technique—in other words, the trails in Naneum Rock Garden are extremely steep, deeply rutted, littered with loose boulders, cut by innumerable tree roots, splattered with cow patties, and guaranteed to challenge the most experienced rider.

Naneum Rock Garden is scenically located on the east side of Table Mountain, overlooking the Naneum Creek drainage and Naneum Meadows to the east and the Yakima River Valley to the west. This entire area is so cut and crosscut by logging roads that the surviving trails have been designated for ORVs. However, because the Forest Service lacks funds to upgrade the area, the trails are unimproved and cyclists will find only limited competition from the motorized users and a bit more competition from equestrian users.

Access: Drive Highway 97 to Swauk Pass. At the summit go east on Forest Road 9716 for 3.7 miles, then turn left on Road 9712. After 1.6 miles turn right on Road 3500 for 0.1 mile, then take a left on Road 3530 and follow it down for 2.3 miles to the trailhead, at the south end of Naneum Meadows (5,040 feet).

MILEAGE LOG

0.0 Start the route by cycling up the Naneum Meadows Trail (No. 1389).

0.2 Go left at a "T" intersection.

0.6 At a "Y" intersection, stay right and continue to follow the Naneum Meadows Trail and continue the very steep climb, which has occasional views east over the Naneum Creek drainage. You will return to this point by The Owl Rim Trail on the left.

1.0 Junction with the Naneum–Wilson Trail No. 1371. Stay to the right and continue up.

2.8 The Naneum Meadows Trail ends. Go left on Road 3500, a well-graded logging road that traverses the crest of Table Mountain.

3.2 Stop at the small roadside turnout for a view west over the Wenatchee River Valley and north to Mt. Stuart. Owl Creek Trail No. 1371B (an alternate route back) is on the left.

3.6 Four-way junction. On the right is Spur Road 124 to Lion

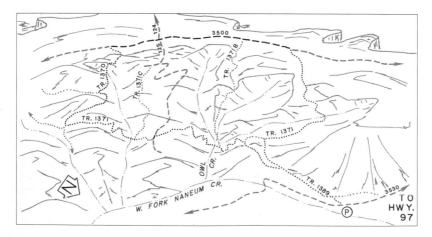

A rail fence marks the precipitous edge on the west side of Table Mountain.

Rock Campground; on the left, Spur Road 125 descends to Drop Creek Spur Trail No. 1371C (an alternate route back). The loop route continues straight ahead on Road 3500, descending through open grassland.

4.6 Turn left and head uphill on Nealy Creek Trail No. 1370. The trail makes a short, rough climb followed by a descent through heavy forest.

5.0 There is a spur road on the right. Pass it without a thought.

5.2 Junction with Regan Jeep Trail No. 1354. Go left, still on the Nealy Creek Trail.

5.5 Junction with Naneum-Wilson Trail No. 1371. Go left on Trail 1371, following signs to Drop Creek. The single-track trail starts out nice and easy for the first 0.5 mile, then makes a sudden Dr.-Jekyll-to-Mr.-Hyde transformation.

7.0 Bottom of the first descent is a junction with the Drop Creek Spur Trail. Stay to the right and descend another 150 yards where the trail joins a logging road.

The rock garden in full bloom

7.1 Go left on the logging road for 75 feet then take a right and return to Trail 1371.

7.9 Begin an elevator drop into Owl Creek.

8.0 Cross Owl Creek to reach the Owl Creek Trail junction. Go straight and push up a very steep slope.

8.2 At a "T" junction (marked by a large rock cairn), go right and follow the trail across a marsh, then north along the edge of the cliffs.

8.7 Junction with the Naneum Meadows Trail. Head right, down along the forested hillside, following the trail back to the start.

8.9 Back at your car, check your brakes and see if you have any rubber left on the pads.

17. Gooseberry Loop

Loop trip: 5.9 miles
Elevation gain: 1,000 feet
Map: USFS: Cle Elum RD
Best: June–September
Allow: 2 hours

Description: road (well maintained); ORV trail (well maintained)
Rating: skilled
Info: Cle Elum RS

Looking for a quick, short ride with lots of zip and kick? The Gooseberry Loop is an excellent choice. The ride starts off with a moderate climb on a well-maintained logging road then follows the route of two ORV trails that twist, turn, and descend like demented snakes back to the start.

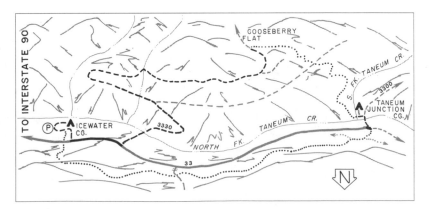

Access: Drive Interstate 90 east of Cle Elum. Leave the freeway at Exit 93 (signed "Elk Hts. Rd."). Go left, cross the freeway, then head to the right following signs to Taneum Creek. In 0.3 mile is a "T" intersection. Turn right and head east, paralleling Interstate 90 for 3.6 miles to the next freeway overpass. Recross Interstate 90 and go right on Taneum Creek Road, which becomes Forest Road 33. Drive up Taneum Creek for 8.6 miles, then turn left into Icewater Campground. Park near the entrance or down by Taneum Creek (2,700 feet).

MILEAGE LOG

0.0 From the campground, ride back up to Road 33. Go left and head upvalley on this dusty and rather busy road for the next 0.2 mile.

0.2 Turn left on Road 3330 then spend the next 0.2 mile descending.

0.4 Once across Taneum Creek the road begins a long, steady climb up the forested hillside.

3.0 At 3,640 feet make a right turn onto Gooseberry Flat Trail No. 1222. (If you reach Gooseberry Flat you have gone 0.1

Descending the Gooseberry

mile too far.) Head down the trail enjoying a smooth tread, interspersed with an occasional rocky section to ensure you don't get too relaxed. The descent is moderate to very steep with a couple of dives to ensure a steady flow of adrenaline.

3.3 The trail crosses a logging road then continues down. It is a brake squealer from this point to the bottom.

4.0 The Gooseberry Trail ends at the Taneum Junction Campground (2,880 feet). Shoulder your bike and rock hop South Fork Taneum Creek or, if it is a warm day, splash across. Once you have crossed the river, go left and ride out to the campground entrance.

4.1 Go right on Road 3300, crossing the North Fork Taneum Creek bridge then crossing the Road (3300)133 intersection. Just past the Road (3300)133 intersection head up a trail that you will find on the left. The trailhead has a sign that indicates you will reach N. Fk. Taneum Trail No. 1377 in 0.5 mile.

4.2 After an amazingly short 0.5 mile, go right on the N. Fk. Taneum Trail No. 1377. This is a double track that receives heavy ORV use.

4.3 Black arrows on orange diamond markers indicate the point where the trail leaves the double track. Head left for a short ascent followed by delightful single-track ride along the hillside.

5.2 The trail crosses a logging road.

5.9 The trail ends at the Icewater Campground entrance. Cross Road 33 then descend on either the road or trail into the campground.

CLE ELUM

18. Frost Mountain Loop

Loop trip: 27 miles
Elevation gain: 2,980 feet
Maps: Green Trails: Cle Elum and Easton
Best: August–mid-October
Allow: 6–7 hours

Description: road (well maintained); ORV trail (very rutted in sections)
Rating: skilled
Info: Cle Elum RS

What kind of mountain bike riding do you prefer—easy roads, rutted ORV trails, forested trails that roll along the valley bottom, steep, rough trails to challenge all your skills? Whatever your choice is, you'll find some of it on the Frost Mountain Loop. Now how about scenery? Take your choice of wide panoramic views, mountain tops, meadows, streams, or cool forests.

This loop is doable by early summer, but, due to deep stream crossings, late summer to early fall (before the hunting season opens and bullets fly) is the best time to ride the loop.

Access: Follow the directions given in Route 17 to Taneum Creek Road. Drive up Taneum Creek Road, which becomes Forest Road 33, for 8.8 miles, then turn left on Road 3330. Find a convenient turnout for parking (2,760 feet).

MILEAGE LOG

0.0 From the start of Road 3330, cycle 0.2 mile down to cross Taneum Creek, then prepare for 7.9 miles of uninterrupted uphill puffing. The road is mostly in forest except for a few openings with views over the Taneum Creek Valley and the Gooseberry Flats Meadow.

6.5 Climbing eases when the road enters Gnat Flat.

8.1 A small saddle at 4,900 feet marks the upper end of Gnat Flat. Now, for a change of pace, the road heads downhill.

8.5 Road 3330 ends. Go right on Road 3120 and continue descending for another 2.2 miles.

10.7 The long descent ends at 4,570 feet. The road now rolls along the ridge crest. Pass several unmarked intersections; continue straight ahead.

12.7 Road 3120 ends after a short descent (4,740 feet). Stay to the right and head up the undulating Road 3100.

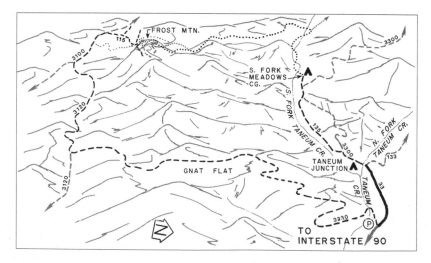

13.7 Pass a 4×4 route which heads steeply up the lower slopes of Frost Mountain to the right. To the left, pass the road access to Frost Meadow (4,810 feet).

13.8 The Frost Mountain Trail heads steeply uphill to the right. Unless your friends have nicknamed you Godzilla for your phenomenal hill-climbing ability, continue on and make your initial climb on a logging road.

14.1 Go right and head up Spur Road 115, which climbs steeply through an old clearcut.

14.6 The road divides at the crest of the ridge; go right.

14.7 The road divides again. Go right on Spur Road 118, which traverses east along the southern clearcut flanks of the mountain. Watch your odometer carefully.

14.9 The Frost Mountain Trail, marked only with a standard issue Forest Service brown fiberglass wand, joins the road from the left. Continue straight ahead on Spur Road 118 for another 0.1 mile.

15.0 Go left on the Frost Mountain Trail, which was marked, in 1994, by a brown wand. The trail switchbacks up the clearcut hillside.

15.1 Trail junction. The Frost Mountain Trail goes left on a low, viewless traverse around the mountain. Unless the weather is terrible, take the right fork and follow Frost Mountain Trail No. 1366A up the hillside through alternating forest and meadows.

15.5 The trail divides again. For now go to the right and continue to ride or push your bike for the final 0.1 mile to the summit.

15.6 Frost Mountain summit (5,740 feet). Take a seat on an old lookout foundation and gaze northeast to the Stuart Range, then eastward to Swauk Pass and Table Mountain. When you are ready to leave, head back the way you came for 0.1 mile.

15.7 Back at the intersection stay right on Frost Water Trail No. 1366B.

16.2 The Frost Water Trail ends; go right on Trail 1366 (5,200 feet), heading downhill. Towards the end of this descent, be prepared for several creek crossings.

19.0 Cycle through South Fork Taneum Creek to join Trail 1367 (3,630 feet). Turn right and cross the South Fork for the second, but not the last, time. Cycle downvalley on a broad, well-graded, rolling trail. Watch out for deep motorcycle ruts in the trail's damper sections.

21.0 The trail ends at South Fork Meadows Campground (3,600 feet). Cycle out the access road for 0.3 mile.

22.3 Turn right on Road 3300 for a short 0.2-mile descent.

22.5 Go right on Spur Road 135, which descends rapidly 0.5 mile to the valley floor, then levels off to parallel South Fork Taneum Creek.

25.1 Spur Road 135 ends (3,200 feet). Go right, back on Road 3300, and continue to descend.

Descending the summit of Frost Mountain

25.6 Coast past the Taneum Junction Forest Camp and across North Fork Taneum Creek, then go right on paved Forest Road 33.

27.0 The loop ends at the Road 3330 junction.

19. Keenan Meadows Loop

Loop trip: 14.9 miles
Elevation gain: 1,080 feet
Map: USFS Cle Elum RD
Best: July–mid-October
Allow: 3–4 hours

Description: road (well maintained); ORV trail (rough and rocky)
Rating: skilled
Info: Cle Elum RS

Four enchanting meadows provide the highlights on this exhilarating loop ride. For most of the summer the meadows are covered with a colorful display of wildflowers. The lucky rider may also spot a deer or elk browsing on the rich, young grass shoots. In late summer and early autumn the meadows' colors turn to warm reds and yellows as cool air descends to halt the summer's growth. Later in the fall the deer and elk wisely disappear, as should all riders, when the hunters invade.

Between the meadows you will ride through forest and clearcuts where the trails are spiked with rocks and ledges, requiring your full concentration and nimble maneuvering. The result is incredible exhilaration when you successfully clear a rough section and delighted chuckles of glee when the trail succeeds in throwing you over your handle bars.

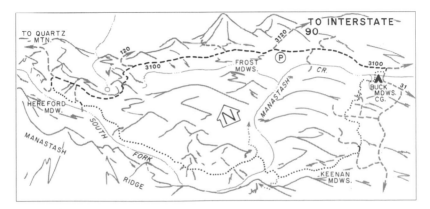

Cruising Hereford Meadows

Access: Follow the directions given in Route 17 to Taneum Creek Road. Drive up Taneum Creek Road, which becomes Forest Road 33, for 8.8 miles then turn left on Road 3330. When Road 3330 ends at 8.5 miles go right on Road 3120 for 4.2 more miles to Road 3100. Find parking on the left near the intersection (4,760 feet).

MILEAGE LOG

0.0 From your parking place begin your ascent towards Quartz Mountain on Road 3100. The climb is steady on a road with an excellent surface. Stick to the obvious route and ignore all side roads.

1.0 Pass the Frost Mountain Jeep Trail on the right and Frost Meadows on the left. These beautiful meadows are a popular campsite during the summer months and an overused hangout for hunters during the fall.

2.4 Spur Road 120 and the Taneum Lake Trailhead are passed on the right (5,440 feet). Beyond this point the road narrows and becomes a bit rougher as the climb steepens.

3.6 Look for a semi-bald hillside on the right (5,800 feet) which has been rutted by 4×4s. A quick walk to the top reveals an unobstructed view to the north where the Stuart Range and Glacier Peak stand tall on the horizon. Road 3100 now follows the forested crest of a ridge, descending, climbing, then descending again.

4.9 Turn left onto Hereford Meadows Trail No. 1207 (5,840 feet). Begin your descent on an abandoned road which races down to an old campsite in Hereford Meadows.

5.1 Once in the meadow the road bends right. At this point, look to your left to find Trail 1207, now a single track, heading down to the lower end of the meadow.

5.7 The single-track trail merges with an old road then continues downvalley, paralleling the South Fork of Taneum Creek.

5.8 Just before the road crosses a creek find the trail on your left. From this point the trail turns into an obstacle course and the fun really begins.

7.1 A short steep climb is followed by a descent back to the edge of the creek.

7.9 The trail climbs away from the creek again.

8.8 Junction (5,130 feet). Following signs to Keenan Meadows go right on Shoestring Lake Trail No. 1385.

9.1 A steep, rough descent leads to a crossing of South Fork Taneum Creek. In early season it is better to log-hop across than to ride. The crossing is followed by a rough, steep climb.

9.5 Intersection (5,080 feet); go left on Keenan Meadows Trail No. 1386 and descend through the meadows. To the right a trail leads to Shoestring

Tiger lily

Lake and Manastash Ridge, a ride that is about as much fun as a broken derailleur.

10.0 Enter Keenan Meadows. Of the four meadows traversed on this loop, this is the most scenic.

10.5 The trail dumps out onto a logging road (4,840 feet). Go left, heading *uphill* on the road.

10.7 Look for an unmarked trail on the right which takes off from the middle of a switchback. Follow this trail as it heads across open clearcuts. This section of the trail crosses a great deal of exposed rock and is a real bone shaker unless you have shocks.

11.0 The trail crosses a logging road then continues its descent.

11.4 The trail meets another logging road and disappears again. Go left for about 50 feet then turn right back on a trail that descends sharply. At the end of the descent, cross a small meadow then enter the forest.

12.2 Cross a seasonal creek.

12.3 Recross South Fork Taneum Creek, this time rolling across a wide, wooden bridge.

12.5 The Keenan Meadows Trail ends at Buck Meadows Campground (4,340 feet). Cycle through the camp area and out to the road.

12.7 Go left on Road 31. After 100 feet you will need to stay left again on the same road, which is now called Road 3100. Head uphill, climbing steadily.

14.9 The loop ends.

CLE ELUM

20. Taneum Ridge Roller

Loop trip: 8.4 miles
Elevation gain: 1,400 feet
Maps: Green Trails: Cle Elum and Easton
Best: June–October
Allow: 2–3 hours

Description: road (well maintained, one steep section); ORV trail (well maintained)
Rating: skilled
Info: Cle Elum RS

The Taneum Ridge ride is similar to a sampler box of Whitman Chocolates—it lets you taste the variety of riding opportunities, more chunky nuts and sticky caramel then cream centers. The loop follows good logging roads up to the top of the ridge, then descends a wide motorcycle trail where you can let go of the brakes

Riding along the South Fork Taneum Creek

and enjoy a lightning-paced ride down in some sections and must slow down for steep rough descents in others. Unlike the other loops in the Taneum environs, this one does not cross a single creek and can be ridden as soon as the snow melts.

Access: Follow the directions in Route 17 to Taneum Creek

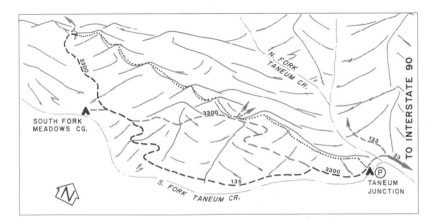

Road. Drive up Taneum Creek Road (which becomes Forest Road 33) for 10.5 miles to a 3-way junction. Turn left on Road 3300, cross North Fork Taneum Creek, and park just beyond at Taneum Junction Forest Camp (2,880 feet).

MILEAGE LOG

0.0 Hop on the bike and pedal up Road 3300. Keep an eye out for traffic on this road.

0.5 Turn left on Spur Road 135, leaving most of the traffic behind. The road descends a little, passing a spur road to a mining claim on the left and an old prospector's cabin on the right.

2.1 Begin a steep climb. The road is rutted and rocky in this section.

2.6 Road 135 ends (3,600 feet). Go left (back on Road 3300) and settle into a steady climb for the next 1.6 miles. Groan.

4.2 The road reaches the summit of Taneum Ridge (4,200 feet). Go right on the Taneum Ridge Trail and cycle along the ridge crest. After 150 feet, the trail merges with an old logging road. Go right, following the crest of the ridge.

Descending the ridge

The Taneum Ridge Trail crosses five forest knolls, requiring five short climbs and five descents in the next 3.3 miles. The first knoll, crossed at 4.8 miles, marks the highest point on the loop. Landmarks viewed from the clearcut crest of this knob include Cle Elum Lake, the Stuart Range, and Glacier Peak.

The trail then descends to a logged-off saddle and crosses another logging spur road. Near the top of the second knoll, the trail enters the forest.

6.7 Emerge from the forest to a confusing array of roads. To the right is Road 3300; to the left are two spur roads. Cycle straight across the first spur road and head uphill on the crest of the ridge to find the trail again.

7.8 Cross another spur road and continue straight down through a clearcut for 100 feet before heading back into the trees.

8.4 The loop ends at Taneum Junction Forest Camp.

CLE ELUM

21. Taneum Creek Waltz

Loop trip: 20.3 miles
Elevation gain: 1,780 feet
Maps: USFS: Cle Elum RS
Best: August–October
Allow: 6–7 hours

Description: road (well maintained); ORV trail (good condition but no bridges)
Rating: skilled
Info: Cle Elum RS

It seems strange that one small valley, in the midst of a land where clearcuts and stumps are the norm, could retain a fresh and pristine feeling. Taneum Creek is an enigma—kind of like one of those forest scenes you see pictured in the magazine ads for chain saws.

The trail down this lovely valley is unique. It was built in an era when men were men and men rode horses and horses could not complain about wet feet when the trail crossed and recrossed a creek. Those of us who eat quiche should take this ride on a warm day in late summer when dancing from stone to stone at each crossing will not seem such a soggy and chilling adventure.

Access: Following the directions given for Route 17, drive to Taneum Creek Road. Head upvalley for 10.5 miles to a 3-way junction. Turn left on Road 3300, cross Taneum Creek, and park at Taneum Junction Forest Camp (elevation 2,800 feet).

The faster the waltz, the drier the feet.

MILEAGE LOG

0.0 From the forest camp ride up well-maintained Forest Road 3300.

0.5 Turn left on Spur Road 135. The road soon divides; stay right, paralleling South Fork Taneum Creek.

2.1 The road becomes steep and rocky.

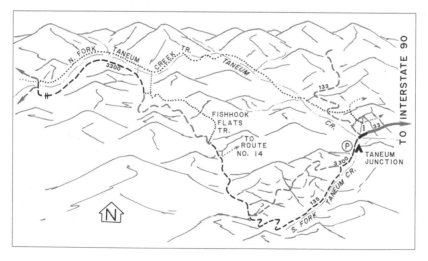

2.9 Road 135 ends. Go left, back on Road 3300, and continue climbing.

4.5 Reach the top of Taneum Ridge, passing the Taneum Ridge Trail (Route 20) on the right.

4.7 Go right on Fishhook Flats Trail No. 1378 (4,240 feet). The trail is delightfully smooth as it descends through the flats, where deer may be seen in the summer and hunters abound in the fall. Beyond the flats the trail climbs over a low hill, then begins a steep descent towards North Fork Taneum Creek.

Thimbleberry

7.0 At the corner of a steeply descending switchback (3,900 feet), look up to the left for an unsigned spur trail. Leave the Fishhook Flats Trail and head up 0.1 mile to Road 3300.

7.1 Back on Road 3300, the descent into the North Fork Valley continues.

10.7 A gate across the road at the edge of a gigantic clearcut blocks automobile access. Cycle around the gate and descend. When the road divides, stay to the right and cross the creek. Head up for 200 feet to the North Fork Taneum Creek Trail No. 1377. Go right, down the valley (4,080 feet). The trail traverses the massive clearcut before reaching the quiet forest, where it starts its dance with the creek.

No attempt is made here to list the creek crossings. You will find them without any help. Enjoy the waltz.

12.0 Pass a spur trail on the right leading to Road 3300.

13.7 Junction with the Fishhook Flats Trail (3,600 feet). Continue down the valley.

18.8 The trail crosses Spur Road 133; ride straight across to regain the trail on the opposite side.

19.5 The trail ends at an old road. Turn right and zip downhill.

20.1 Hang a sharp right at the bottom of the descent and head onto a narrow trail that leads to paved Road 33.

20.2 The trail ends at an intersection. Go right on Road 3300 and cross a bridge. The loop ends at Taneum Junction Forest Camp.

22. Lookout Mountain Loop

Loop trip: 12.0 miles
Elevation gain: 1,700 feet
Map: Green Trails: Easton
Best: June–mid-October
Allow: 3–4 hours

Description: road (well maintained); trail (good condition, steep and rough in sections)
Rating: skilled
Info: Cle Elum RS

Seven mountains in the state of Washington have the double distinction of bearing the name "Lookout Mountain" and of having fire lookouts on their summits. However, when it came time to place buildings on appropriately named mountains, the Lookout Mountain in the Taneum Creek area was overlooked. Today the summit of this Lookout Mountain is as untouched as when it was named by some optimistic forester.

The loop ride around Lookout Mountain is both scenic and challenging. The loop starts by following a gated logging road up through a massive clearcut to an ORV trail. The trail traverses the crest of an open ridge, skirting steep cliffs and traversing alpine meadows, then ends with a fast-paced descent through forest to the clearcut valley floor.

Access: Follow the directions given in Route 17 to Taneum Creek Road. Drive upvalley for 10.5 miles to a 3-way junction. Go left on Road 33 and follow it for 11.2 miles to a gate in a giant clearcut (4,000 feet).

MILEAGE LOG

0.0 Cycle around the gate, down to a "Y," and go right. Cross the North Fork Taneum Creek bridge, then start to climb. About 200 feet beyond the bridge, the North Fork Taneum Creek Trail crosses the road. (You will return to this spot at the end of the loop by the trail on the left.) A few feet beyond the trail crossing

Rider near Lookout Mountain

Rider descending to Windy Pass

the road divides again; stay left for the long switchback climb into an upper basin. The road crosses Lookout Creek, then climbs into another drainage.

1.4 The road crests a half-clearcut saddle (5,160 feet) where you will find Trail 1326 on the left, clearcut side, of the hill. Make a 180-degree turn and head steeply up on Trail 1326, looking down on the road you were just on. The rocky trail rolls

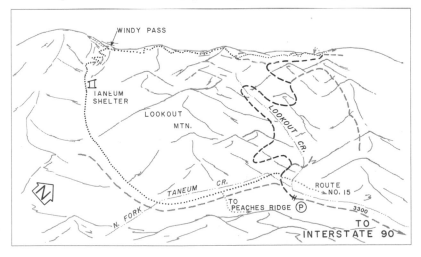

along the ridge crests making several, short, steep ascents.

5.7 The trail crosses a logging road then climbs steeply for the next 0.3 mile before leveling out to open meadows and views.

6.3 Extreme caution is needed as the trail crosses to the north side of the ridge. For the next 15 feet the trail crosses bare rock. This is a very exposed area and it is best to walk your bike.

6.9 The trail leaves the ridge (at 5,700 feet) and heads steeply down toward Windy Pass. Before descending, take time to look at the view or walk to the crest of a small knoll on the right for a view that includes Mt. Adams and Mt. Rainier and everything in between.

7.4 Windy Pass (5,280 feet). Go left (south) and descend a rutted trail into the forest.

8.3 At the edge of a meadow, pass the Taneum Shelter (4,600 feet). The shelter is a mess, with cans and garbage left for the forest creatures to harvest. Beyond the shelter the descent moderates and the trail winds through forest.

9.8 Cross North Fork Taneum Creek and enter a massive clearcut. The trail climbs illogically and steeply, then descends into a band of trees. From this point on, the trail is in poor condition and the creeks are without bridges.

10.8 Peaches Ridge Access Trail is passed on the right.

11.2 The trail brushes a road.

11.5 Cross North Fork Taneum Creek, which is deep and wide in early summer.

11.8 The trail meets the road. Turn right on the road and recross the North Fork Taneum Creek bridge.

12.0 The loop ends at the gate.

ENUMCLAW

23. Evans Creek Loops

Loop trip: up to 9.6 miles
Elevation gain: up to 1,500 feet
Map: Green Trails: Mt. Rainier West (trails not shown)
Best: mid-June–October
Allow: 2–8 hours

Description: roads (moderately maintained); 4×4 roads (steep and rutted); trails (steep and narrow)
Rating: moderate to skilled
Info: White River RS

Evans Creek is an ORV area located just west of the Mowich Lake entrance to Mt. Rainier National Park. It's a small area laced with logging roads, 4×4 routes, and motorcycle trails. Unless you

Trail 1148 has an excellent view of Mt. Rainier.

are looking for a truly easy ride, you can find a route you'll enjoy here. If you are looking for challenge, the Evans Creek area is guaranteed to provide it. If it's views you want, Mt. Rainier can be seen on most loops. For skilled riders it is an excellent place to challenge yourself. For the adventurous it's an ideal place to fine-tune your ability to ride the nearly vertical.

Access: Drive to Buckley on Highway 410, then go south on State Route 165 heading towards Wilkeson and the Carbon River. The road passes through Wilkeson after 4 miles. Continue south another 5.6 miles to the one-lane bridge over the Carbon River. In 0.5 mile beyond the bridge, the road divides; go right toward Mowich Lake for 8 miles (mostly on gravel road). Turn left on Road 7920 and drive 1.7 miles to a major intersection. Stay to the right on Road 7930 for 30 feet, then take a left into a large parking area (3,500 feet).

MILEAGE LOG

Listed below are six short loops of varying difficulty. Pick one that sounds good and head out. If the loop is too hard or too easy, try another.

Loop 1 (Rating: moderate)

This is the easiest loop, with all but 1 mile on logging roads. One section of the descent is steep and rough, but for the rest of the loop the roads are well graded. Views are excellent of Mt. Rainier to the south and Tacoma, Seattle, Puget Sound, and the Olympics to the west. The loop is 9.6 miles long and gains 1,100 feet.

0.0 From the parking area pedal east up Road 7930, passing a 4×4 route, the campground, and a motorcycle trail.

1.4 The road divides; go left and continue climbing.

2.3 The road divides; take the left fork and head west.

3.7 Reach a saddle with excellent views, then follow the main road to the right.

4.2 Leave the road at a second saddle (4,600 feet) and go left on 4×4 Route 519.

4.9 The 4×4 route divides; continue straight ahead on 4×4 Route 519.

5.2 4×4 Route 519 ends. Descend a steep, abandoned logging road.

6.0 Abandoned road ends. Go straight ahead on nearly level Road 7920.

6.9 Intersection; go left, still on Road 7920, and descend gradually back to the parking area.

9.6 End of Loop 1.

Loop 2 (Rating: moderate)

This loop follows a logging road and a 4×4 route. The logging road is well graded; however, the quality of the 4×4 route varies from steep and sandy to smooth and level. Most riders will enjoy this loop. The steep sections are short and may be easily walked. It's a 5.7-mile loop with a 900-foot elevation gain.

0.0 From the parking lot, head east up Road 7930.

1.4 The road divides; go right and begin a steady climb up to the ridge crest.

2.0 At the top of the ridge the road divides (4,400 feet); go right (downhill).

2.2 The road ends. Continue down the ridge on 4×4 Route 311. The 4×4 route is very steep at the beginning but soon moderates. Avoid all spur roads or trails on the left (they lead to logging roads on the south side of the ridge).

2.9 Intersection with a 4×4 route from the campground. Go left and continue to follow the ridge, avoiding spur trails on the left and watching out for bottomless mud holes.

4.0 4×4 Route 311 ends. Go right on Road 7920 for an easy cruise back to the start.

5.7 The loop ends at the parking lot.

Loop 3 (Rating: skilled)

This is a fun road-and-trail loop. If you enjoy forested trails with a lot of twists and turns, you'll enjoy this 5.1-mile loop with only 500 feet of elevation gain.

0.0 Head west from the parking area on Road 7920. The road is rough with little elevation gain.

1.3 At a wide corner, leave the road and descend to the left on Trail 1140.

View of Mt. Rainier from Road 7930

1.5 Trail 1140A branches off to the right. Continue straight.

2.5 Intersection; go left to 4×4 Route 102 (3,040 feet.)

2.6 The road crosses Evans Creek (don't count on a bridge here). Shortly after the creek, go left on Trail 1153, which climbs steadily.

3.4 Go left on Road 7920 for a nearly level ride back to the parking area.

5.1 End of Loop 3.

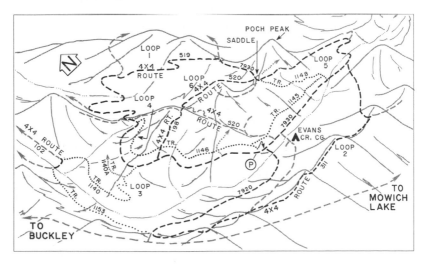

Loop 4 (Rating: skilled)

This is another road-and-trail loop. The road portion is easy; the trail portion is challenging but not difficult. The loop is 5.2 miles long with only 300 feet of elevation gain.

0.0 Cycle west from the parking lot on Road 7920.

2.5 Go right on Trail 1146. The trail climbs for the first 0.4 mile, then settles into a series of short descents and shorter climbs. The trail is wide and well graded as long as it is in the forest and narrow and rough in the clearcuts.

3.5 The first of three 4×4 routes crosses the trail.

3.8 A spur trail branches off to the right and descends to Road 7920.

5.2 Intersection; go right and descend to the parking lot.

Loop 5 (Rating: skilled)

Another road-and-trail loop. The climb is on well-graded road and the descent on narrow, rough trail with sharp and deeply rutted corners. The loop totals 5.9 miles with an elevation gain of 900 feet.

0.0 Cycle east from the parking lot on Road 7930, passing a 4×4 route, the campground, and a trailhead.

1.4 At the end of the valley the road divides; go left.

2.3 The road divides again; take the left fork and head west along the flanks of Poch Peak.

3.7 The road enters a broad saddle (4,400 feet) and divides. Check out the views of Mt. Rainier and the Puget Sound lowlands, then head down Trail 1148, which starts on the left just before the road divides. The trail drops down through a clearcut, switchbacking and occasionally, for no particular reason, climbing steeply.

5.0 Intersection; go right (west) on Trail 1147, which parallels Road 7920. (If you go left here you will reach Road 7920 in 0.1 mile.)

5.4 Junction with Trail 1145. Continue straight ahead, winding over and around the trees, rocks, marshes, and streams.

5.7 Cross 4×4 Route 520.

5.9 Go left and descend to the parking area.

Loop 6 (Rating: skilled)

This 8.9-mile loop is a challenging combination of well-graded logging road and rugged 4×4 route. Elevation gain is 900 feet.

0.0 From the parking area, head east on Road 7930 for 3.7 miles to a saddle (for details of the first 3.7 miles, see Loop 5).

3.7 At the far (northwest) side of the saddle, go west on 4×4 Route 520.

3.9 Trail 1145 branches off to the left; continue straight.

6.7 After several switchbacks, go right on a well-defined 4×4 route.

6.8 Join 4×4 Route 198 and go left for a breathtaking drop downhill, keeping left at all intersections.

7.6 Go left on Road 7920 and coast gently back to the parking area.

8.9 End of loop.

HIGHWAY 410—WEST

24. South Grass Mountain Road Loop

Loop trip: 15.7 miles
Elevation gain: 2,280 feet
Map: USFS: White River RS
Best: mid-June–September
Allow: 4–5 hours

Description: road; some steep and poorly maintained sections
Rating: moderate
Info: White River RS

If you enjoy outstanding scenery, save this ride for a crystal-clear day and treat yourself to a 360-degree view that starts and ends with Mt. Rainier.

Almost the entire area covered on this loop has been logged with only a few remaining stands of mature trees guarding the ridgetops. While the new tree plantations are maturing the roads in this area will receive only limited use and limited maintenance. Vehicle traffic on these roads is light, except during hunting season.

In mid-June the clearcuts at the top of Grass Mountain are covered with bear grass.

Access: Drive Highway 410 east from Enumclaw 16.6 miles to Federation Forest State Park. Go right and drive to the parking area. Restrooms and water are available (1,640 feet).

MILEAGE LOG

0.0 From the parking area ride back to Highway 410.

0.1 Turn left and ride downvalley on Highway 410.

1.9 Take a right on Forest Road 7120 and begin the long, at times grueling, climb up Grass Mountain (1,520 feet). Pass two unmarked spur roads on the right.

3.3 The road divides (2,400 feet); stay right on Weyerhaeuser Road 6303 (Forest Road 7120) and continue to climb.

3.5 The grueling portion of the climb is over; the road levels then rolls along the crest of the ridge.

3.6 Pass the first of five spur roads on the right and three on the left. (Stay on Weyerhaeuser Road 6303 at all intersections.)

6.8 The road crosses over a spur ridge on a narrow saddle at 3,520 feet with a great view.

7.7 Spur Road 210 branches off to the left.

7.9 Go left on Weyerhaeuser Road 6407 (also Forest Road 225) and follow as it climbs to the ridge crest then drops a few feet to a logged-off saddle.

8.5 From the saddle on the rolling crest of Grass Mountain (3,900 feet), walk up the hill to the east for a view from the summit. Find a perch and slowly rotate to take in the entire view (like dining at the Space Needle except you do the turn-

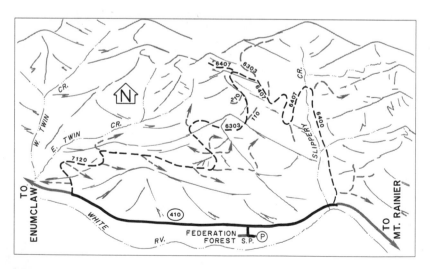

ing yourself). After a couple of rotations walk back to your bike and descend back to the intersection of Road 6303 and Road 6407.

9.1 Go left; it's all downhill from here.

9.4 Turn right following Weyerhaeuser Road 6407 (Forest Road 310) and drop into the Slippery Creek drainage. This poorly maintained road descends rapidly and you will want to hang on tight to the brakes. Pass several spur roads; at each intersection take the obvious road heading down.

12.3 Cross Slippery Creek.

12.4 Weyerhaeuser Road 6407 ends. Continue your descent on Road 6400.

14.2 Pass a major intersection, stay right and continue to descend.

14.4 Weyerhaeuser Road 6400 ends at Highway 410. Go right and end your loop with a ride along the paved shoulder of very busy Highway 410.

15.0 Enter Federation Forest State Park.

15.6 Make a careful left turn across Highway 410 back to the state park visitor center.

15.7 Loop ends at the parking area. If you have any spare time, treat yourself to a HIKE (no bikes allowed on the trails) along the White River through the venerable old forest.

25. Naches Cliff

Loop trip: 13.5 miles
Elevation gain: 1,920 feet
Map: USFS: White River RS
Best: mid-June–October
Allow: 4–5 hours

Description: 4×4 road (very rough and sandy); forest road (well maintained)
Rating: skilled
Info: White River RS

Pioneers were tough, determined people. For a small taste of what early settlers went through to reach the milk and honey of the Puget Sound area, take a ride on the old Naches Wagon Trail. The crux of the trail was the drop down Naches Cliff, where the pioneers lowered their wagons on ropes and scrambled down with the oxen on foot.

Today the Wagon Trail is overrun by jeeps and motorcycles, and clearcuts have replaced the dense forest that covered the area when the pioneers passed through. But the terrain is still the same, with the cliff as a reminder of how the pioneers worked where we now play. As you bounce down the old wagon trail on your high-tech mountain bike, remember those who traveled over the same ground, covering perhaps 5 miles a day with their oxen and wagons.

The Naches Cliff ride covers the wagon trail route on the west side of Naches Pass to the top of the cliff. The route follows well-graded logging roads up to Government Meadow. The descent is on 4×4 routes and motorcycle paths along the route of the Naches Wagon Trail and is very steep and rough in sections. In order to preserve the famous cliff, that section of the trail has been closed to all but hikers. Mountain bikers must return to the road here. Everyone, however, should walk up the cliff and take a look.

Access: From Greenwater drive east on Highway 410 for 2 miles then go left on Forest Road 70. Follow this paved road up the Greenwater River Valley for 8.7 miles then take a right on Road 7033 and follow the signs to the Greenwater Lake/Naches Trailhead (2,480 feet).

MILEAGE LOG

0.0 Okay you pioneers, mount your steel ox and whip it back down Road 7033. Turn right on Road 70 and head uphill.

6.3 The road divides. Continue straight ahead on the narrower of the two roads (Road 70), ignoring the well-used road on the left (Road 7080).

7.0 When the road divides a second time, go left and head steeply uphill on Spur Road 260.

7.1 The road bisects the Naches Wagon Trail. Look for a wide 4×4/motorcycle road signed Naches Trail No. 1175. Turn left

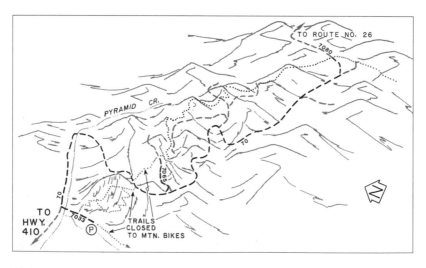

Descending the Naches Wagon Trail

onto the trail (4,000 feet) and start down through meadows and clearcuts. Expect ruts, loose rock, and rough log bridges.

8.0 The trail crosses Road 7080 and heads out along the ridge crest.

8.6 Cross an unmarked road.

8.8 Cross another unmarked road.

9.3 Cross yet another road where the route splits into many directions but stick with the obvious downhill. Don't worry about picking the wrong trail; they all merge lower down.

10.4 Unmarked 4-way junction; go straight, heading downhill. The left fork ends in 75 yards. The right fork is a nasty 4×4 route.

10.9 The trail reaches Road 7065. From this point on the trail is closed to wheeled vehicles. Go left and continue your descent on the road.

11.1 Road 7065 ends. Go right on Road 70 and descend along the top of the Naches Cliff.

11.2 Pass a rocky spur on the left side of the road. The view from the top is excellent.

13.3 Turn left on Road 7033.

13.5 The loop ends at the base of the trailhead parking area. Before you pack it up and head home take time to walk the trail up the cliff. A sign tells of the troubles the pioneers experienced here.

26. Wagons Ho

Loop trip: 19.7 miles
Elevation gain: 1,900 feet
Map: USFS: White River RD
Best: April–October
Allow: 5–6 hours

Description: road (well maintained); 4×4 road (rutted, steep, loose rocks, and dirt)
Rating: skilled
Info: White River RS and Naches RS

In the mid-1800s, pioneers living in the Puget Sound area built a wagon trail from Walla Walla to Steilacoom. The trail crossed the Cascade Range at Naches Pass. They hoped this trail over Naches Pass would attract more settlers into the area; however, only a couple of wagon trains, some warring Indians, and a few cattle herders ever used it. The trail was too difficult.

Until recently, a few vestiges of the old Naches Wagon Trail were visible, such as the wheel ruts left by the wagons. Today, there remains only a churned-up swath crossing the pass, rutted and scarred by an overdose of 4-wheel-drives and motorcycles. However, you can still get a feel for the old trail by riding the route over Naches Pass traveled by the pioneers on the way to their own Acres of Clams.

This loop route covers the east section of the Naches Wagon Trail, the easier of the two sides to ride. (See Route 25 for a description of the west side.) The ride starts near Government Meadow, crosses Naches Pass, then descends 8 miles down the east side. On the way, plan to encounter the same sand, loose

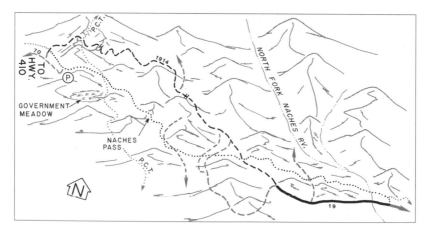

rock, roots, mud, ruts, and steep hills the pioneers encountered. To facilitate the return, you may follow logging roads back to the west side.

Access: Head east from Greenwater on Highway 410 for 2 miles. Turn left on Forest Road 70. At 15.6 miles go left on Spur Road 260 and head uphill for 0.1 mile to a rough parking area where the trail crosses the road (4,700 feet).

MILEAGE LOG

0.0 Go right and ride uphill through a logging clearing on a well-maintained 4×4 route signed as the Naches Wagon Trail. Before long the trail enters the forest and you must work your way around mud holes and over rough corduroy.

0.5 Cross the Pacific Crest Trail. To the south lies Government Meadow, a scenic oasis in the dense forest.

1.1 Summit of Naches Pass (5,000 feet). The route heads down the east side first through picturesque meadows with the summit of Mt. Rainier just visible on the southwestern horizon. Beyond the meadows, the trail descends through a large clearcut.

1.6 Cross a logging road.

Modern pioneers are still looking for a better route over Naches Park.

4.5 Cross Road 1914 and continue down.

5.7 The first of three unmarked logging roads is crossed. The other two spurs will be crossed in the next 0.2 mile.

7.0 The Wagon Trail crosses the North Fork Naches River. Pioneers forded the river; cyclists may do the same. Or you may follow the trail to the right, crossing a small creek on a wide wooden bridge then cycling on out to Road 1913. Go left passing the Middle Fork Naches ORV trailhead on the left then crossing a solid cement bridge.

7.2 Shortly after crossing the bridge, turn right, back on the Naches Wagon Route. This lower section of trail begins by circumnavigating a giant mud-wallow created by 4×4s at play.

7.4 Go straight across a logging spur road. Watch for deer and elk in this section.

8.6 The trail divides; stay to the right and follow a motorcycle trail around a low hill. The two trails will rejoin in 0.2 mile. The next section of trail heads down the nearly level Little Naches River valley. The valley floor is sheltered by a dense forest cover and the trail is muddy, unpleasantly muddy, impossibly muddy.

9.1 The 4×4 route divides; stay to the left and continue downvalley.

9.2 Go right and escape the mud by following a faint spur road for 10 feet to reach the edge of paved Little Naches River Road No. 19 (3,200 feet). Turn right and ride upvalley to the end of the pavement. The road has no shoulder, so use caution.

13.3 Go right, heading uphill, on Road 1914.

13.9 The wagon trail crosses the road. Soon after, the road begins a mile-long descent.

15.5 Pass a road gate (almost always open) dividing Plum Creek land from Forest Service land. Shortly thereafter, stay left at an unsigned intersection.

16.4 Reach a low saddle and a major intersection. Head to the left on Spur Road 787. The road is level for nearly a mile and then begins a long, switchbacking climb over the crest of the Cascades. Pass numerous spurs but stay on the most used road.

18.5 Pass a gate and reenter Forest Service land. A few feet beyond, the Pacific Crest Trail joins the road for the final climb to the ridge crest.

18.8 At the crest of the ridge the Pacific Crest Trail heads off on the right, climbing the clearcut hillsides as it heads toward Snoqualmie Pass. The road descends then climbs to a second ridge crest.

This sign tells the whole story.

19.4 Second summit and view overlooking the start of the ride. Go left and follow a steep ORV trail high up on the hill then head straight down an old logging clearing toward your starting point.
19.6 The trail ends on Spur Road 260. Go left to return to your car.
19.7 End of loop.

HIGHWAY 410—WEST

27. Dalles Ridge Loop

Loop trip: 22.8 miles
Elevation gain: 3,270 feet
Map: USFS: White River RD
Best: late June–September
Allow: 5–6 hours

Description: road (well maintained); trail (narrow and steep)
Rating: skilled
Info: White River RS

Wow! What an excellent loop! The views are excellent, the roads are excellent, and the trails are excellent.

This excellent loop over Dalles Ridge can be divided into three sections. The first part of the ride is a scenic 10.2-mile ascent on well-maintained forest roads from the floor of the White River valley to the crest of Dalles Ridge. Riding this section of the loop requires no skill, just a lot of energy and appreciation of the views of Mt. Rainier. The second portion of the loop is a series of three trails that bring you back down to the valley floor. These trails are not for the timid rider. They are narrow and the tread is full of large rocks and roots. Switchbacks are sharp, often requiring riders to get off and lift their bikes around the turn. The final section is an easy 3.3-mile ride on the paved shoulder of Highway 410.

Access: Drive Highway 410 east 5.8 miles from the Greenwater General Store then turn left on Forest Road 72 for 0.1 mile. Park in the small turnout just before the gate (2,080 feet). (The turnout is large enough for one car. Additional parking can be found on the spur road to the left of the turnout.)

MILEAGE LOG

0.0 Starting at the gate, ride up Road 72. Views and that burning feeling in your legs begin immediately as you climb above the valley floor.

0.2 Unmarked intersection; stay right. Road 72 wanders on and off Forest Service land. Spur roads on private lands are not marked. Stick with the best-looking road at all intersections and you shouldn't go wrong.

2.5 Intersection and progress report. Stay left on Road 72 and continue to climb; the worst is behind you now.

4.8 The road crosses from the west to the east side of Dalles Ridge, then heads south just below the crest.

7.6 Major intersection. Turn right and ride uphill on Road 7250. Road 72 descends into the Greenwater River Valley.

9.7 Go left on Spur Road 210 and continue south along the ridge.

10.2 Dalles Ridge Trail No. 1173 (unsigned) begins as a cat track

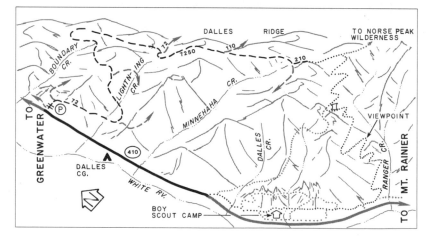

Photo taken at a peaceful moment before the rider cart-wheeled down the hillside and body-slammed into a tree (Sorry, Chip, I had to tell.)

from the end of the road. Follow the cat track over a knoll to its end, then ride straight ahead on an obvious path. After 500 feet the path leaves the clearcut and becomes a wide trail which rolls along the west side of Dalles Ridge.

10.8 In the middle of a steep hillside, make a sharp right on Ranger Creek Trail No. 1197 (5,370 feet) and begin a long descent. This trail is used by the occasional hiker, so keep an eye on the route ahead and a hand on the brakes as you descend. The trail soon drops down into the timber.

12.0 Just beyond a messy hikers' shelter is an intersection with the Palisades Trail. Stay left and continue the descent on Ranger Creek Trail. Use caution; the trail is full of hazards such as rocks, roots, sharp corners, and hidden stumps. Be sure to give the occasional hiker the right-of-way.

12.2 The trail divides; go right and climb above a small slide area.

14.0 Little Ranger Creek Viewpoint. Leave your bike and walk the 0.1-mile spur trail over a rocky knob to a view of the White River valley, Fawn Ridge, Crystal Mountain, Castle Mountain, and Mt. Rainier.

16.4 The Ranger Creek Trail ends (2,600 feet). Turn right on White River Trail No. 1199. This forested trail parallels Highway 410 and is heavily used by Boy Scouts and mountain bike riders. Ride with caution.

16.7 A short side trail descends to Highway 410; continue straight ahead.

17.7 Intersection; pass the Buck Creek Trail on the left and, 20 feet beyond, Snoquera Falls Trail on the right.

18.0 A 4-way intersection. Trails on left and right belong to the Boy Scouts and are closed to mountain bikes.

18.1 The trail divides; stay right, passing above the Scout camp.

18.3 On the north side of the Scout camp the trail divides again; continue straight.

18.4 The White River Trail ends temporarily on a grassy slope. Descend to the powerline road, and follow it for 15 feet to find the trail again on the right.

18.8 Cycle straight through another 4-way intersection.

19.1 The Palisades Trail joins the White River Trail on the right. Stay left and descend steeply.

19.2 Intersection with the Powerline Horse Trail; go right and continue the descent toward the valley floor.

19.4 The White River Trail ends at Highway 410 (2,300 feet). Go right and cycle down the White River valley on the paved shoulder of Highway 410. Use caution—the shoulder of this busy road narrows without warning.

22.7 Turn right, back on Forest Road 72.

22.8 The loop ends at the gate.

A cloudy day view from Sun Top Mountain Road

HIGHWAY 410—WEST

28. Sun Top Loop

Loop trip: 22.9 miles
Elevation gain: 3,340 feet
Map: USFS: White River RD
Best: July–mid-October
Allow: 7–8 hours

Description: road (well maintained, steady climb); trail (steep, rough, very difficult)
Rating: skilled
Info: White River RS

If you like hard climbs, difficult trails, and endless challenges when you're mountain biking, the Sun Top Loop is your kind of ride. The loop starts off with a "leisurely" 7 miles of road, in which you climb a mere 3,200 vertical feet. That's the easy part. It's the following 15 miles that require real skill and endurance on the part of the rider. The trails have numerous natural obstacles such as roots, rocks, and sandy soils. You are also challenged with artificial hazards like narrow tread, ruts, steps, and bridges.

This is a very scenic loop, with close-up views of Mt. Rainier from the ridgetops and beautiful old-growth forest on the valley floor.

Access: Drive Highway 410 east from the town of Greenwater for 6.6 miles. Turn right on Forest Road 73 and descend for 0.3 mile. Cross the White River and park just beyond the bridge, opposite the Skookum Flat Trailhead (elevation 2,100 feet).

MILEAGE LOG

0.0 Start the loop by riding up Forest Road 73. Ride defensively, as you'll encounter considerable traffic on this road. Look out for tourists, berry pickers, hunters, the U.S. Army on training missions, and loggers.

0.5 Cycle past a large experimental seed farm.

1.0 At the end of the seed farm, turn left on Road 7315 and begin climbing to the lookout. You will pass several spur roads; stick with the obvious main road. The climb is relentless; the occasional views are excellent.

5.9 Pass the Sun Top Trail on the left. A few feet beyond is a saddle and a junction (4,760 feet). Go right, still following Road 7315 for the final grind up to the summit.

6.8 The road ends at Sun Top Lookout (5,270 feet). Mt. Rainier is the chief attraction here, dominating a quarter of the horizon. Crystal Mountain Ski Resort, Noble Knob, Huckleberry Ridge, Huckleberry Mountain, and Green Mountain also occupy the horizon. After snapping a few pictures (and eating a bucket of huckleberries in season), descend to the saddle. The true start of the Sun Top Trail is from the summit; however, the upper portions are unrideable so stick to the road.

7.7 Back at the junction, go left for 50 feet, then take a right on Sun Top Trail No. 1183. The trail heads south along a forested ridge and climbs for the first mile.

8.9 Break out of the trees to an open ridgetop at 5,440 feet. Stop to enjoy the view; it is the last grand 360-degree look on the loop. The trail now begins a roller-coaster descent along the ridge.

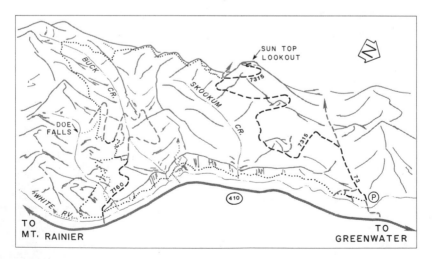

A sunny day view from Sun Top Mountain

11.4 Cross Buck Creek and begin descending. Stop once in a while to appreciate the views of the White River valley.

12.5 Ride across Road 7160 (4,400 feet) and continue your descent.

12.8 The trail divides; stay left. The right fork is a hiker-only trail that contours south ½ mile to Doe Falls.

13.2 The trail is again intersected by Road 7160. Turn right and ride 75 feet down the road to find the trail on the right, half-way around the first corner. Head down to a messy camp area where the trail divides. Stay right and continue down.

13.4 The trail meets a logging spur road and ends. Follow the road to your left for 50 feet then find the trail on the right and head down the steep hillside.

14.4 Spur Road 310 cuts across the trail. Cross the road and head right for a few feet to rejoin the trail. The trail descends then contours south to Doe Creek. The creek is forded then the trail descends again.

15.0 The trail divides; go right. Watch for horses with inexperienced riders, often kids, in this section.

15.4 The trail is bisected by an old, somewhat overgrown road. Go straight ahead with a slight right bend. Yes, this is a confusing area.

15.5 At an obvious "Y" intersection, go left and descend a steep hill. At the bottom you will cross an often dry creek bed and shortly beyond arrive at a multi-intersection. Go right then take the first left and ride out to Spur Road 210.

15.7 Turn right on Spur Road 210 and head south for 200 feet to a sharp bend. Leave the road here and go left through a gravel-covered parking area to find Skookum Flats Trail No. 1194. Follow this trail to the left and head downvalley along the White River. The Skookum Flats Trail is no picnic. This nearly level trail twists and turns, crossing endless roots and occasional rocks. Intersections are too numerous to note. Always head downvalley and follow the most obvious trail.

17.3 The trail goes right on an old road. Before long the road divides; stay left.

17.4 The trail ends temporarily on Road 7160. Go left for 30 feet to find the Skookum Flats Trail on your right (2,480 feet). This trail will return you to your starting point in 5.4 difficult miles. A brief log of the trail follows below (for full details see Route 29). *ALTERNATE ROUTE:* If continuing down this difficult trail no longer sounds appealing or you are running short on time, cross the White River and follow Highway 410 downvalley to Road 73. This shortcut will reduce the riding time by 2 hours.

18.6 The White River Trail divides at the swing bridge. Go left, uphill, on the river trail.

18.9 The trail divides; stay to the right.

20.6 Cycle across the Skookum Creek bridge, below Skookum Falls.

22.1 The trail enters a selectively logged area. Cat roads and jeep trails wind through the trees in inexplicable directions. The trail is easy to follow; it is the only track too narrow for a jeep.

22.9 The White River Trail reaches Road 73, and the loop ends.

HIGHWAY 410—WEST

29. White River Rambler

Loop trip: 11.0 miles
Elevation gain: 500 feet
Map: Green Trails: Greenwater
Best: March–November
Allow: 4–5 hours

Description: trail; obstacles of all varieties
Rating: skilled
Info: White River RS

Don't be fooled by the low mileage and lack of significant elevation gain on this loop—it's a very challenging ride. The majority of the ride is on a trail that bends, twists, and bounces. Along the way you will beat your bike over rocks and huge tree roots, then meander around sharp bends where a missed turn means a deadly plunge into the river. In short, this ride is a technical thrill.

The only really dangerous portion of the loop is on Highway 410. Traffic is almost always heavy and, although the broad shoulder offers some protection, some drivers of large vacation vehicles would, in a pinch, rather sacrifice a cyclist than spill their beer.

Access: Drive Highway 410 east from the small town of Greenwater for 11.7 miles and turn right on Forest Road 7160. Cross the White River to reach the Skookum Flats Trailhead, located on the right just a few feet beyond the bridge. Drive 200 feet past the trailhead and park in a handy turnout (elevation 2,600 feet).

MILEAGE LOG

0.0 From the turnout, cycle back to the trailhead (now located on your left). The start of the trail is wicked, offering a taste of all the challenges to come. If the first 0.2 mile is not fun, this is not the ride for you.

0.2 A trail from a horse camp joins on the left. Stay to the right, heading downriver. The riding becomes a bit more relaxed and the obstacles are spaced farther apart. The trail enters a section of the White River valley untouched by loggers. This narrow section of primitive forest is dark and lovely.

1.2 The trail crosses Buck Creek, then divides. Take the left-hand fork, heading steeply uphill; the right-hand fork leads

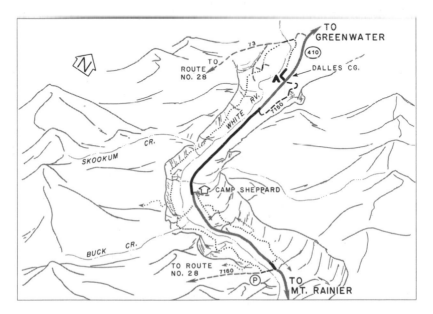

The trail weaves through old-growth cedars

     to a suspension bridge over the White River, then on to Camp Sheppard (a Boy Scout camp).

1.5 The trail divides again. Take the lower of the two trails; the upper goes to the Buck Creek Horse Camp.

3.2 Skookum Creek bridge. Beyond the bridge a rough footpath climbs uphill for a view of Skookum Falls. The falls disappear in dry weather, so don't spend a lot of time searching in late summer.

4.7 A confusing intersection marks the end of the protected valley bottom. The trail now passes through an area of selective logging. The forest floor is laced with old cat tracks, spur roads, and jeep trails. At this first intersection go straight across a jeep road to find the trail on the opposite side. A few feet beyond is another road; follow it until a wide trail takes off on the right.

5.4 The trail ends (2,100 feet). Turn right on Road 73 and cycle across the White River bridge.

5.5 Ride 30 feet beyond the bridge, then look uphill on the right for pipeline markers and a trail. The trail is well graded and easy to follow.

6.0 The pipeline trail ends near the large Douglas fir at the southern end of Dalles Campground. Go right and follow the campground road out to Highway 410.

6.5 From the campground entrance, cycle straight across Highway 410 to Forest Road 7150. Pass a community of vacation cottages before descending back to the highway.

7.6 It cannot be avoided: go left on Highway 410.

9.3 Turn left at the Camp Sheppard entrance. Just before the gate, go right on an old forest road paralleling the main highway.

9.6 The old forest road/trail divides; go left, following signs to the White River Trail.

9.7 When the trail meets a road, turn right for 50 feet and then left, back on the trail again.

9.8 Trail junction. Go right, cycling upvalley on the White River Trail. This trail has a good tread with a few steep ups and downs.

10.8 At a thoroughly signed junction in a logging cut, turn downhill to Highway 410. At the highway, take a left. Ride upvalley to the Road 7160 turnoff.

11.0 Cross the White River and pass the Skookum Flats Trailhead to reach the starting point at the handy turnout.

HIGHWAY 410—WEST

30. Crystal Mountain Loop

Loop trip: 13.1 miles
Elevation gain: 2,872 feet
Map: Green Trails: Bumping Lake
Best: mid-July–September
Allow: 6–7 hours

Description: road (maintained); trail (steep and rough)
Rating: skilled
Info: White River RS

At Crystal Mountain Ski Resort you can try the European approach to a day in the mountains. After a hard ride to the top, order lunch at the summit restaurant, then relax on the sun deck and enjoy a view that includes Mt. Rainier, Mt. Adams, and Mount St. Helens before you head down.

This ride is for strong, experienced riders only. The 6.1-mile climb from the valley floor to the summit of Crystal Mountain is entirely on trail. The climb is gradual and much of the trail is rideable by strong cyclists. If you have more money then strength, the chairlift is available all summer to sweep you and your bike up to the high point. The descent is on rough, narrow, exposed trail. The only easy portion of the ride is the final descent on a road down the valley from the resort to the trailhead.

Riders on the trails in the Crystal Mountain area must be ready to deal with horses and their (possibly) inexperienced riders at all times. When you see a horse, pull off the trail or to the side of the road. Talk continuously to let the horses know you're just a human with a bicycle.

Access: Drive Highway 410 east from Enumclaw. At the Mt. Rainier National Park boundary, turn left on Crystal Mountain Road and follow it for 4.8 miles. After crossing Silver Creek for the second time, turn right on Spur Road 510. After 0.4 mile, pass a spur road to an informal camping area on the right. Continue straight to the end of the road and the Crystal Mountain Trailhead (elevation 4,160 feet).

MILEAGE LOG

0.0 Begin the 2,872-foot climb up Crystal Mountain on a well-graded trail which ascends the steep hillside, sometimes through forest, sometimes across open meadow.

3.1 When you reach the ridge crest (6,400 feet), stop and enjoy the view over the White River valley to Mt. Rainier. The trail now follows the ridge south, gaining elevation as it climbs over three hills.

3.5 An unmarked trail branches on the left; continue straight ahead.

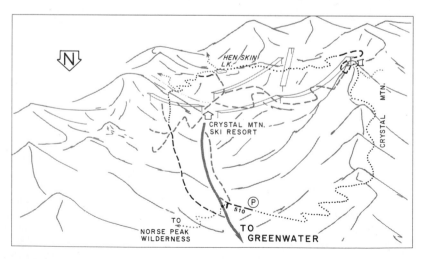

4.7 Unmarked intersection; go right.

5.3 Cross the Crystal Mountain ski area boundary.

5.6 At Elk Pass the trail turns into a cat track for the final ascent to the summit. Numerous spur trails branch off on both sides of the cat track; ignore them.

6.1 The summit of Crystal Mountain (6,970 feet) is adorned with a chairlift and a restaurant. Spend some time on the terrace of the Summit Restaurant and enjoy the outstanding view. Heavy-wallet riders will start their adventure from this point.

Climbing the Crystal Mountain Trail

In the summit area you must use extra caution to weave your way through the camcorder crowd; their reaction times are slow away from the motorhome. When the smell of fresh cologne and cigarette smoke gets to you, head down on the road that parallels the chairlift.

6.3 At Tower No. 14, turn right on a rough service road which crosses under the chairlift, contours around the mountain, then descends along a ridge crest.

6.7 When the road ends continue straight ahead on a trail that makes one switchback down the open hillside. Skirt along the lower edge of the basin then head south across the open meadows below Silver Queen. Watch out for the tourists who rode the chairlift up and are walking down on the trail.

7.5 Enter Campbell Basin, pass under two chairlifts, and cross a cat track (6,120 feet).

7.8 The trail crosses a service road then splinters in several directions. Keeping the creek on your right, go straight until you intersect the road a second time. Go right and follow the road downhill for 75 feet. Just before the road crosses a small creek, go right on a trail that fords the creek then heads uphill into the woods.

8.2 Pass a couple of small lakes.

8.4 Cross a small creek; no bridge.

8.7 The trail divides above lower Hen Skin Lake (5,730 feet).

Descending toward Hen Skin Lake

Go left and descend to the lake, then follow the wide trail around the lakeshore.

8.8 On the north side of the lake, head into the trees on a broad trail.

8.9 The trail ends at the edge of a wide cat track; go right. In 100 feet the cat track divides; stay right.

9.0 The cat track ends; continue straight on a trail.

9.2 Intersection with a second trail from Hen Skin Lake. Go left and descend rapidly through dense forest.

9.5 Jim Town, the site of an old miner's camp (5,590 feet). Stay left and continue to descend.

10.4 The trail crosses a creek, passes an abandoned mine, heads across a ski slope, then ends (4,800 feet).

10.6 Turn left and descend a ski area service road.

10.9 This is a junction of four roads and one trail. Head down then to the right on a well-traveled road which heads north, down the valley.

12.9 Pass the Norse Peak Trailhead on the right. Continue down the road another 200 feet then go left on a rough horse trail.

13.0 Cross paved Crystal Mountain Road then follow the trail on down to the camp area. Ride across the camp area and head up the access road.

13.1 Go left on Road 510 to end your loop at the Crystal Mountain Trailhead.

31. West Quartz Creek Loop de Loops

Fife Ridge

Loop trip: 16.7 miles
Elevation gain: 2,480 feet
Map: Green Trails: Old Scab Mountain
Best: July–mid-October
Allow: 3–4 hours
Description: road (well maintained); ORV trail (steep, loose rocks)
Rating: skilled
Info: Naches RS

West Quartz Creek

Loop trip: 14.4 miles
Elevation gain: 1,900 feet
Maps: Green Trails: Old Scab Mountain and Easton
Best: July–mid-October
Allow: 3–4 hours
Description: road (well maintained); ORV trail (loose rocks and sand)
Rating: skilled
Info: Naches RS

You get two, two, two loops in one. The first loop, Fife Ridge, is the one for the scenery-minded, with views of Mt. Rainier, American Ridge, and Manastash Ridge. The second loop, West Quartz Creek, is a romp through the forest with only a brief view now and then. Both loops start with easy rides up logging roads and end with fast-action, white-knuckle descents on trails. Best of all, you can do both rides without moving your car. This is a popular motorbike area, so start early to avoid the competition.

Access: Drive Highway 410 east 23.5 miles from Chinook Pass, then turn left on Little Naches Road for 2.7 miles. Take a left on

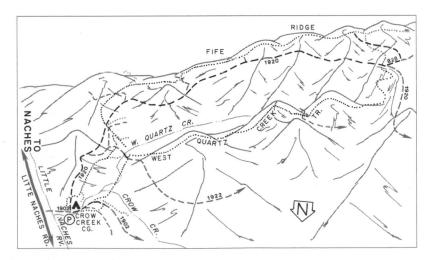

Forest Road 1902 and follow it 0.4 mile to a "Y" intersection with Road 1920. Go straight ahead and find a large parking area at the center of the "Y" (2,800 feet).

FIFE RIDGE MILEAGE LOG

0.0 Your loop begins with a long uphill grind on Road 1920. As you pedal past the first corner, take note of the ORV trail on the right; you will return by this trail.

1.1 Pass a junction with Road 1922, stay left, and continue on Road 1920. Several other spur roads will branch off as you climb; ignore them and stick with Road 1920.

1.6 Trail 952 (your descent route) crosses the road at 3,400 feet.

4.6 A short trail connects Road 1920 with your descent route. It is possible to head down here; however, a lot of good trail riding will be missed.

6.1 The road descends for the next 1.7 miles.

7.8 West Quartz Creek Trail No. 952 crosses the road (4,700 feet). From this point you have two options. Either push your bike up Trail 952 for 1 mile or, an easier choice, follow this mileage log and cycle up Spur Road 828, which starts on the left after you cross the trail.

8.2 Take a left turn on Spur Road 829. Ride over the berm that has been created to keep vehicles out then head on up the road.

Dive, dive, dive . . .

9.0 Trail 952 crosses Spur Road 829. Continue on the road.

9.8 Road 829 ends with a spectacular view. After absorbing as much view as you can head out to your right on an old cat road. After 150 feet you will find a rough motorcycle trail which will take you to the edge of Fife Ridge.

9.9 When you intersect Trail 952, take a left turn and begin your descent. For the next 6.8 miles you will almost forget what pedals are for; however, brakes will always be on your mind. *Note:* The trail is rough and rocky for the first 1.6 miles then smooths out in the lower sections.

10.0 Pass through a clearcut then head into a white-knuckle descent.

11.5 The trail comes within 100 feet of Road 1920, then crosses a spur road. Continue straight ahead.

11.8 Skirt along the crest of vertical cliffs. Mt. Rainier can be seen to the west.

13.0 The trail passes through several clearcuts near the edge of the cliffs. There are more views here, but who has time to look on a descent as fun as this one?

14.2 Arrive at a "T" intersection. Go left, still on Trail 952. After 100 feet the trail crosses a road then heads steeply down to cross a seasonal creek.

14.9 Cross Road 1920. You have seen this place before.

15.1 The trail divides; stay to the right and head across an old spur road.

15.2 The trail divides again; stay to the right.

15.3 Cross Road 1922 and continue down.

16.0 Your unmarked trail will merge with another unmarked trail. Stay to the right and continue the descent on a wide track with lots of berms to hop.

16.4 Go right when your trail divides on a steep, open hillside.

16.5 Cross Road 1920 for a final downhill plunge.

16.7 Your trail ends at the edge of Road 1902. If you did everything right, your car and Road 1920 should be to your left. Now head back up for the West Quartz Creek Loop.

WEST QUARTZ CREEK MILEAGE LOG

0.0 Follow the Fife Ridge Mileage Log for the first 7.8 miles to the intersection with West Quartz Creek Trail No. 952.

7.8 Starting at 4,700 feet, let go of the brakes and head down Trail 952. The descent starts off with a couple of switchbacks, then traverses across an exposed slope, a good place to get the hands back on the brakes. From this point on, descent is fast so watch out for areas where the tread of the trail suddenly deteriorates to either loose rock, loose sand, or loose rock and sand. There are three short, steep climbs that let you relax, push the bike, and shake out the hands.

9.4 Cross an old logging road and begin the biggest climb of this wonderful descent. After 0.4 mile the downhill fun resumes.

10.2 The trail crosses a logging road. A second road is crossed after another 2.3 miles.

13.1 A descent down a rocky slope ends with a splash as you cross West Quartz Creek. After 0.2 mile the trail will recross West Quartz Creek.

13.4 A wooden bridge provides a dry crossing over Crow Creek.

13.6 At the intersection with Trail 963 go right. After a 50-foot climb you will reach Road 1902. At this point you may choose an easy 0.4-mile descent down Road 1902 back to the start or you may go left, up the road, for 200 feet and join Trail 963 then go right and descend on trail.

13.9 When Trail 963 divides, stay to the right. Cross Road 1921 then follow the trail down to Crow Creek Campground. Hop on the road and ride past the campground entrance then cross Crow Creek.

14.4 The loop ends at the parking area next to the Crow Creek bridge. You got two, two, two loops in one.

HIGHWAY 410—EAST

32. Sand Creek Wild Slide

Loop trip: 15.2 miles
Elevation gain: 1,420 feet
Maps: Green Trails: Lester and Easton
Best: mid-June–October
Allow: 3–4 hours

Description: road (well maintained); ORV trail (well maintained)
Rating: skilled
Info: Naches RS

In mankind's never-ending search for the ultimate thrill, some travel to the ends of the earth to ski the perfect powder slope; for others it's a continual safari to surf the glassiest waves; while many thrive on a ceaseless hunt for the best gourmet coffee. Now, Sand Creek may not be the ultimate mountain bike ride, but this researcher believes it comes mighty close. The trail is wide and well packed, the corners are banked, and the downhill grade is just right for an all-out descent. Views are interesting but not overpowering enough to distract you from your ride.

Access: Drive Highway 410 east from Chinook Pass to the Little

Naches Road. Go left and head upvalley 2.7 miles; go left on Forest Road 1902 for 0.4 mile. When the road divides, go straight to a large parking area at the center of the "Y" and park near Crow Creek (2,800 feet).

MILEAGE LOG

0.0 Ride across the Crow Creek bridge to an intersection on the far side then go left, still on Road 1902. The well-graded, hard-surfaced road climbs steadily up the forested hillside. ***ALTERNATE ROUTE:*** You may stay right at the intersection and follow the lesser used Road 1921, adding an extra 2 miles to the total.

0.4 Pass the West Quartz Creek Trail, and after 100 yards pass the Sand Creek Trail. You will see this point again on your way back down.

4.1 The climb ends and the road levels off, then descends a bit.

5.2 Road 1921 joins Road 1902. Continue on up Road 1902.

6.1 Sand Creek Trailhead and a camp area on the left (3,610 feet). It is an informal camp area with no signs and a shaky pit toilet. Ride into the upper end of the campsite where you will find trail signs. Two trails begin here. Trail 963, which begins at the upper end of the camp area, is the traditional trailhead and the one followed in this mileage log. Trail 963A is an alternate, shorter trail which begins at the center of camp. Trail 963 starts by heading upvalley, paralleling the road, and climbing gradually. Several small creeks are crossed, including Sand Creek, some with bridges and some without.

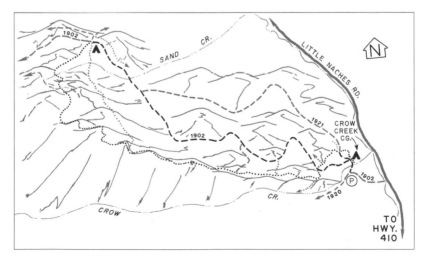

Take a ride on a wild slide.

7.8 The trail begins to climb and soon after crosses a logging road.

8.9 On a 4,220-foot knoll the trail reaches the highest point of the ride. The only brake-pad burning of the entire descent occurs shortly after you start down.

9.5 Trail 963A appears from over the hill.

10.8 Views pop in and out of sight for the next 1.5 miles. Unless you are a fan of forested hills there is not much to look at anyway, so keep your speed up.

12.2 A slight uphill puts a short break in the action.

13.8 At 3,200 feet there was a logging road on the left, or were you flying by too fast to see it?

14.3 The trail divides; stay right (the left fork goes out to Road 1902).

14.6 The trail divides again; take the left fork and cross Road 1902.

15.0 The trail divides again; stay right, following the ridge.

15.1 The trail crosses Road 1921. Follow the road for 100 yards, then drop down a rough trail to Crow Creek Campground.

15.2 There is probably time to do it all over again.

33. Lost Meadow Loop

Loop trip: 13.0 miles
Elevation gain: 2,000 feet
Map: USFS: Naches RD
Best: July–mid-October
Allow: 4–5 hours

Description: trail (steep sections, deeply rutted, loose rock); 4×4 road (amazingly steep sections)
Rating: skilled
Info: Naches RS

Before heading out on this ride, take time to answer the following simple questions: Do you like to shake, rattle, and roll? Do you like climbing steep hills just for the pleasure of going down the other side? Do you enjoy sweating and swatting bugs? Are you addicted to trail riding?

If you can answer yes to all the above, then you are sure to love the Lost Meadow Loop. If you are looking for views and mellow cruising, this is not the ride for you.

Access: Drive Highway 410 east from Chinook Pass (or west from the town of Naches) and turn left (northwest) on the Little Naches Road. Follow this paved forest road for 8.4 miles then take a left on South Fork Road No. 1906. After 0.3 mile go right on Spur Road 686 (very rough) and descend to a large, graveled parking area (3,120 feet).

MILEAGE LOG

0.0 From the start it is important to understand that there is nothing easy about this loop. Just finding your way out of the parking lot is a challenge and route finding remains

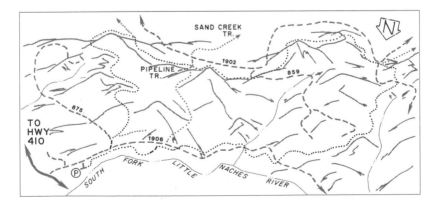

difficult for the first 0.4 mile. Find a trail at the upper left-hand side of the parking area. Begin at the trail sign and bear left, ignoring all other trails. Your trail will parallel the road. A spur trail branches left; ignore it. When the trail divides, stay left.

0.4 The trail reaches Road 1906. Ride across the road then take an immediate left on Spur Road 875.

0.5 When Spur Road 875 bends to the left, go right and ride or walk up a steep bank that has been well churned by wheels. At the time of this research the trailhead was unsigned.

0.7 *Important:* The trail divides; stay left and climb steeply for 0.1 mile before you get a chance to catch your breath. The forest floor, covered by a glowing carpet of lupin, is truly beautiful. The trail, covered with knobby roots, is not even pretty.

2.6 The trail descends through a selective timber cut then crosses a spring (3,500 feet).

3.6 Cross a 3,880-foot ridge crest then descend around the edge of a large clearcut.

4.3 The trail meets the Pipeline Trail (a double track used by 4×4s) and ends (3,630 feet). You won't waste time here reading signs; there are none to be seen. Go right and begin a rolling climb along the forested ridge on a road that parallels the underground phone lines.

4.6 Road 1902 can be seen a few feet below. It looks very inviting.

4.7 Pass Clyde's Hole. Clyde and his jeep may still be in there.

4.9 Intersection (3,670 feet). To the left is a small forest camp and the Sand Creek Trail (see Route 32). To the right an ORV trail offers an alternate, faster return to the starting point. Your route continues straight ahead—that is, unless you choose to prove that mountain bikers have brains as well as muscles by abandoning the Pipeline Trail and riding Road 1902 for the next section. The road was not surveyed, but it looked excellent—now what does that say about the author?

5.1 Cross Spur Road 862.

6.3 At 4,180 feet the Pipeline Trail crosses Spur Road 859. Continue straight ahead for the steepest climb of the loop.

7.4 The Pipeline Trail crosses a rocky 4,860-foot summit then heads down. The descent is followed by two more short climbs.

8.1 A major intersection marks the end of your trial-by-knee-abuse on the Pipeline Trail. To the left is Road 1902. The Pipeline Trail crosses a spur road then continues straight. You should go right on South Fork Trail No. 946 and begin

Still looking for Lost Meadow

your descent back to the South Fork Little Naches River with an easy climb.

8.3 At 5,110 feet you begin your descent. Cross an old road and head down the single track through open forest.

8.4 The trail crosses a small creek. Watch for deer and elk.

9.1 Begin an elevator drop down a deeply rutted hillside.

9.5 The trail climbs over a low ridge (4,470 feet) then continues its descent.

10.5 The South Fork Trail crosses South Fork Road No. 1906 (3,640 feet). Road 1906 is now paralleled back to the start.

11.1 The trail recrosses Road 1906.

11.6 Cross the road for the last time.

11.8 The trail merges with an old road and descends to the river. After a short glimpse of the South Fork the old road ends and the trail climbs back to Road 1906.

11.9 At the ridge crest the trail divides; stay left and ride along the ridge.

12.1 The trail merges with another old road; continue straight.

12.4 The trail brushes along the edge of Road 1906 then returns to the forest.

12.6 The loop portion of the ride ends and you now follow your outgoing tracks back to the parking area.

13.0 It's over. Go ahead and join the motorcycles for a run up on the gravel pile before heading home.

34. Little Naches Valley Roller Coaster

Loop trip: 17 miles
Elevation gain: 860 feet
Map: USFS: Naches RD
Best: June–October
Allow: 3–4 hours

Description: road (paved); ORV trail (rough with loose rock)
Rating: skilled
Info: Naches RS

If you want an adrenaline-pumping, hair-raising, thrill-a-second roller-coaster ride the Little Naches Valley Trail is the place to go. A paved forest road allows you to quickly complete your ascent to the trailhead, ensuring plenty of time for the return on a wide trail designed for motorcycles. The trail offers shade but no views as it dips and climbs as if following the path of a hyperactive squirrel.

Strong riders, with thighs as big as old-growth cedar trees, can ride the entire loop. However, most cyclists will have to push up several of the steeper climbs.

Access: Drive 23.5 miles east from Chinook Pass on Highway 410 then turn left on Little Naches Road. After heading upvalley for 2.6 miles turn right on an unmarked, paved road. (This is the first road on the right after Kaner Flat Campground.) After 150 feet you should find a large parking area (2,800 feet).

MILEAGE LOG

0.0 Return to Little Naches Road and go right, heading upvalley on pavement. This is the most scenic section of the ride as the road passes through meadows then parallels the river.

1.2 The road enters a narrow canyon, where it crosses the river twice. To the right is a viewing platform overlooking a small cascade.

1.5 Pass Longmire Meadow and an access to the Little Naches Valley Trail on the right. You will pass several more trail accesses as well as spur roads that access the trail as you head up the valley.

4.6 Pass the Mt. Clifty Trailhead at Fourway Meadow.

5.7 The road crosses the Little Naches River then recrosses it in 0.3 mile.

7.5 A large, detailed map on the right-hand side of the road indicates that it is time to turn around and head back downvalley. Your trail begins across the road, paralleling your upvalley route (3,160 feet).

7.8 The trail merges with the road and shares the bridge over Cub Creek. You then must cross the road and return to the trail for a ride over a grassy meadow.

7.9 Pass a junction with Trail 943. Continue straight ahead on Trail 941, cross Road 1911, then head into the forest. You now are ready to start on the roller coaster. Use caution to avoid catching a pedal where the trail is deeply rutted.

8.2 Cross another logging road.

9.6 One hundred feet after crossing a bridge over a swampy creek you will arrive at an unmarked intersection. Stay to the left and ascend yet another low hill.

10.6 The trail crosses a logging road then continues on its forest ramble.

10.7 Cycle straight across the Mt. Clifty Trailhead parking area.

11.7 A steep, winding, and very bumpy descent takes you to a bridged creek crossing. Professional rodeo riders don't have this much fun.

12.2 Pedal along the edge of a swampy lake. You will want to use a great deal of energy here in mosquito season.

13.1 A steep descent leads to a parking area at the edge of the paved Little Naches Road. Enjoy a brief moment on level ground before heading up yet another hill.

13.8 At the top of a 3,000-foot hill is an unmarked "T" junction. Go right and descend steeply along the edge of a small meadow.

14.2 After a short, steep descent the trail crosses a logging road at a sharp corner.

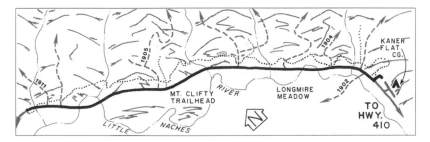

Another "zooming down the trail" photo

14.6 The trail divides. Continue straight ahead. To the right is Longmire Meadow.

14.8 The trail crosses another logging road.

15.7 A trail merges from the left. Go right and descend to a lightly forested meadow where you will cross another logging road.

16.0 Junction of Trails 949 and 941. Stay right and descend to the trailhead parking area for Trail 949. Head through the parking area, cross Road 1903, then bear down for your last climb. When the trail reaches the ridge line it divides. Follow the trail that bends sharply to the left and continues climbing for another 0.2 mile.

16.9 At the end of your descent, cruise over level ground toward Little Naches Road. About 10 feet before you reach the pavement go left on an unmarked trail.

17.0 The end.

35. Little Bald Mountain Loop

Loop trip: 30.7 miles
Elevation gain: 3,608 feet
Map: Green Trails: Old Scab Mountain
Best: July–September
Allow: 6–7 hours

Description: road (maintained, rough in sections); ORV trail (good condition)
Rating: skilled
Info: Naches RS

View watching is the chief hazard on the Little Bald Mountain route. Riding the well-graded logging roads up the mountain or descending the wide ORV trail is no problem, if you can keep your eyes on the route ahead. Trouble is you are plagued with outstanding views for almost the entire ride. The views start early and get grander as you climb. When you reach the summit, the site of Little Bald Mountain Lookout, you may think you have seen it all. But then you head down the trail and find the most thrilling views of all, from the edge of tall cliffs—which brings us back to the trouble of watching where you're going. (Part of this problem may soon be solved as the Forest Service plans to move the trail away from the cliffs and out of the wilderness, oops.)

Access: Drive Highway 410 east 23 miles from Chinook Pass. Turn right on Forest Road 1704 and pass an informal and unsigned camp area then cross the American River and find a convenient place to park (2,380 feet).

MILEAGE LOG

0.0 The road divides just after crossing the bridge. Go right and head uphill on (unsigned) Forest Service Road 1709. After the first couple of miles the initial steady climb abates and this well-maintained road heads into an endless, gradual, but steady grind along the forested hillside. Intersections and spur roads are common; stay on the obvious main thoroughfare.

3.4 First view of Little Bald Mountain; it's the cliffy knob rising above the trees ahead. Manastash Ridge fills the eastern horizon.

4.7 Road 1791 branches off to the right. Stay left on Road 1709, which is nearly level in this area, and wind through the forest plantations.

8.2 Road 1709 meets Road 1706 and ends. Continue straight ahead on Road 1706 (3,600 feet).

9.8 Pass the Lost Creek Trail on the left.

13.3 Road 1706 ends (4,600 feet). Stay right and continue the climb on Road 1600. The road surface quality begins to deteriorate as you climb briskly. The road leaves the forest and enters subalpine meadows.

15.0 Pass the Little Bald Mountain Trail. The trail starts from a small saddle at 5,350 feet, directly below the summit. Even if your legs feel like jelly, keep going. The best views are found at the top.

16.2 Turn right on Spur Road 231 for the final 0.4 mile to the top.

16.6 Summit of Little Bald Mountain (6,108 feet). A solar-powered radio antenna stands on the site of the former lookout tower,

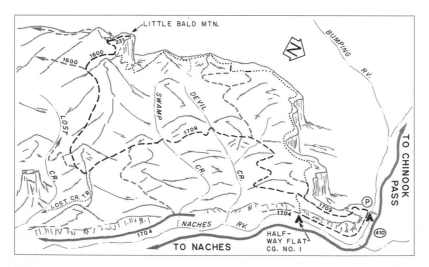

Crossing a boulder field on Little Bald Mountain

which was burned accidentally in 1980. Find a comfortable vantage point away from the edge of the cliffs and enjoy the view. Mt. Rainier and Mt. Adams dominate. To the west rise Old Scab Mountain, Goat Peak, and American Ridge. Fife Ridge to the north leads the eye out to a multitude of summits like Bears Breast, Hinman, Daniel, and Mt. Stuart. To the east lie Bald Mountain and Yakima. To the south you'll see Bethel Ridge and the Goat Rocks. When ready, glide the 1.6 miles back to the trailhead.

18.2 The trail starts in the trees on the right side of the saddle, switchbacks down the cliff, then heads out over a large rock field.

20.3 Reach an open ridge with excellent views (5,300 feet).

21.1 At 4,740 feet the trail reaches a logging road. Turn left and head downhill on the road for 0.2 mile.

21.3 Pick up the trail again at the second corner, on the left-hand side of the road.

21.5 Cycle through a narrow band of trees to another road at the top of a large logging clearing. Jog left on the road for 15 feet to rejoin the trail.

22.0 Cross unmarked trail. *Note:* The following mileages may change in the future as the trail will be rerouted out of the wilderness. The changes should be well marked and easy to follow, causing only a slight change to the overall mileage total.

22.2 The trail reaches a rocky ridge and disappears on the crest. Cycle straight along the crest until the trail reappears.

22.3 Cross a jeep road and continue straight. For the next 5 miles the trail skims along the top of the cliffs that plunge down to the Bumping River. The trail surface alternates from loose rock to looser sand. Keep your speed down and cycle in control. Watch where you're going! Do not attempt to admire the view and ride at the same time.

27.6 The trail ends at a logging road. Turn left and cycle downhill for 0.8 mile to road's end.

28.4 Spur road ends at Road 1709. Go right for 75 feet. The trail, unsigned, is on the left side of the road, starting from a small mound of dirt.

29.3 The trail ends at Old River Road and Halfway Flat Campground No. 1. Go left and follow the road north along the Naches River.

30.7 The ride ends at the American River bridge.

HIGHWAY 410—EAST

36. Bald Mountain Loop

Loop trip: 14.0 miles
Elevation gain: 1,540 feet
Map: Green Trails: Manastash Lake
Best: June–September
Allow: 3–4 hours

Description: road; varies from well maintained to rough, steep, and rutted
Rating: moderate
Info: Naches RS

If you are blasé about incredible views, open ridgetops, forested lakes, and sculptured sandstone, this ride will seem quite ordinary. Most mortals, however, find this area absolutely extraordinary.

The route over Bald Mountain follows roads over its entire distance and is very challenging. The ride starts on well-maintained logging roads, then branches off onto rocky and rutted 4×4 routes. Be ready for steep climbs and even steeper descents.

Access: Drive Highway 410 east 33 miles from Chinook Pass or west 14.3 miles from the junction of Highways 12 and 410. Turn east on Rock Creek Road No. 1702. An unmarked spur road branches off on the right at 2.6 miles; stay left. At 3.7 miles from Highway

410, the road divides and you need to take the right fork, Road 1720. Follow Road 1720 for 5.3 miles to a "T" intersection at the crest of the ridge. Park off the road near the intersection (4,460 feet).

MILEAGE LOG

0.0 From the "T" intersection head north (left) across grassy meadow lands at the top of the ridge on Forest Road 1701 (the road number sign may be missing). The road climbs up a 5,080-foot knoll, descends briefly, then climbs again. Several signed and unsigned spur roads are passed; ignore them.

2.4 Turn left on Spur Road 530 (5,780 feet) and begin the climb up Bald Mountain. The road is graded but the surface is covered with loose rock. The climb starts in trees and soon breaks out onto a grass- and flower-covered hillside. Mt. Adams, the Goat Rocks, and Divide Ridge are in view.

2.5 Pass a 4×4 route on the left heading straight up the hillside. Stay on Road 530.

3.2 An unmarked road branches off to the left. Stay right and continue climbing.

3.5 The road divides again when it reaches the crest of the ridge. Go left. Shortly beyond, the road splits again; either fork works.

3.9 Bald Mountain Lookout site (5,850 feet). Countless hills and ridgetops spread out before you in a broad panorama. Spur Road 530 ends here and Summit Trail No. 644, a rugged 4×4 road, begins. Follow Trail 644 northwest along the ridge

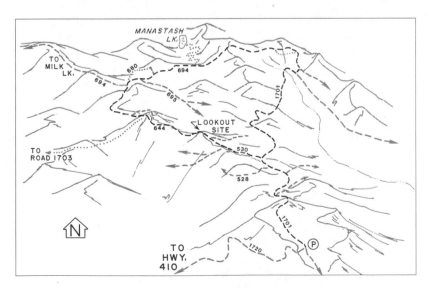

crest. The trail will split and rejoin numerous times as it descends to a saddle then climbs the next knoll.

4.5 Part way up a steep hill the trail divides. Take the left fork and cycle around a sparsely forested hill to a broad meadow-covered bench.

4.7 Gold Creek Trail, unsigned, meets the Summit Trail and ends.

5.6 Summit Springs Junction (5,850 feet). Go right on Trail 694 and head toward Manastash Lake. Trail 694 soon divides; stay to the right and climb up and over the crest of the ridge.

5.8 Trail 695 branches off to the left. Your trail, No. 694, makes a sharp turn to the left. ***SIDE TRIP:*** If you have some spare time for exploring, make a short excursion out on Trail 695 to look at the sandstone formations.

6.0 Pass Trail 699, which heads straight up to the ridge crest. If you have time to explore, consider heading up the steep slope for a view from the top. Beyond the Trail 699 intersection you will descend past sandstone formations reminiscent of Utah.

6.3 The 4×4s have created routes that go over or around a shoulder of a large sandstone formation. Spend some time here practicing your slick-rock skills then head up over the sandstone.

Sandstone formation near the Manastash Lake junction

6.7 **SIDE TRIP:** A motorcycle trail drops over the north side of Manastash Ridge to Manastash Lake, 600 feet below. The 0.7-mile trail is steep but rideable. The return trip will be a push.

The loop route continues to follow the ridge.

7.0 Trail 698 branches off to the right; stay on Trail 694, which follows the crest of the ridge. Watch for views north to the Stuart Range, Hinman, Daniel, and Bears Breast.

7.9 The road divides; stay left.

8.7 Two hundred feet after passing the Trail 696 intersection go right on Trail 670 and head straight downhill. Grab your brakes; you are going to need them.

8.9 Trail 670 reaches Road 1701 (5,000 feet). Go right (west) on Road 1701 for an easy climb back to the ridge crest.

11.6 Pass Spur Road 530 on the right, ending the loop portion of the ride. Now descend to the start.

14.0 Road 1720 signals the end of your ride.

37. Bethel Ridge

Bethel Ridge

Round trip: 8.4 miles
Elevation gain: 400 feet
Map: Green Trails: Rimrock
Best: July–mid-October
Allow: 1–2 hours
Description: road (well maintained); jeep road (rough)
Rating: moderate
Info: Naches RS

Loop Ride

Round trip: 17.2 miles
Elevation gain: 2,300 feet
Map: Green Trails: Rimrock
Best: July–mid-October
Allow: 4–5 hours
Description: road (well maintained); jeep road (requires route finding and bushwhacking)
Rating: adventurous
Info: Naches RS

Towering high between the Tieton and Naches Rivers is a mountain bikers' paradise called Bethel Ridge. Riders need pedal only a few miles along the ridge to hear the whispering of the pines, smell the sweet sage, and obtain astounding views. The 4×4 trail followed on this route skirts the edge of a 1,000-foot drop-off, and the unobstructed views are awesome.

Two rides are suggested here. The Bethel Ridge ride takes in the most scenic section of the ridge, climbing up to Observation

141

Point on a well-maintained forest road then following the crest of Bethel Ridge for several miles beyond on an easy 4×4 route.

The Loop Ride is strictly for riders who love adventure, demanding riding, great scenery, and sweat. This ride follows 4×4 trails and mixes elevator-drop descents with a long push up a roadless and trailless hillside.

Access: Drive Highway 12 east 18 miles from White Pass. Turn left on Bethel Ridge Road No. 1500 and drive uphill for 7 miles to the ridge crest. Park in one of several small turnouts near Spur Road 324 (5,600 feet).

BETHEL RIDGE MILEAGE LOG

0.0 Cycle up Spur Road 324. The road surface is solid, with a coating of crushed gravel. Expect some car traffic here.

2.1 At 6,180 feet, near the summit of Bethel Ridge, Spur Road 324 turns left into the trees toward a group of radio towers. Continue straight ahead on Spur Road 325 for 50 feet to Observation Point. The views extend over the Tieton River Valley and Rimrock Lake to Divide Ridge and Mt. Adams.

2.3 The road divides; stay right paralleling the edge of the cliffs. Descend to a broad saddle then climb up to a rounded knoll.

4.2 The top of the rounded knoll (6,000 feet) is a good spot to stop for a picnic under the shady trees before heading back. From this point the road and ridge descend rapidly.

LOOP RIDE MILEAGE LOG

0.0 Follow the Bethel Ridge Mileage Log for the first 4.2 miles.

4.2 From the top of the rounded knoll (6,000 feet), continue east on Spur Road 325. The road leaves the cliffs and descends rapidly through forest and open meadows. Watch for grouse, deer, and elk.

4.3 Climb a short hill and pass a hunters' camp.

4.5 Ignore a spur road on the left and continue your descent.

6.7 This is the trickiest part of the loop. At 5,440 feet a poorly defined, unsigned 4×4 trail branches off to the right. The trail is only faintly visible as it heads out over open sage at the upper edge of a large meadow. (If you reach a junction with road signs, you have gone 0.6 mile too far.) Once on the 4×4 trail, head straight across the meadow. At the far side of the meadow, bear left and follow the 4×4 trail as it drops down the south side of the ridge.

7.6 The 4×4 trail ends on Spur Road 235. Directly across the road, Spur 676 heads down a short hill to the Lynne Lake camp area (4,580 feet). When ready, go left and descend Spur Road 235.

Bethel Ridge

8.2 At the second spur on the right *below Lynne Lake,* go west on Spur Road 236 (4,300 feet). Cycle up a pretty valley, across a basalt field, then over a wooded ridge.

10.4 The maintained road ends at a "Y" intersection (4,850 feet); go left on a rough, unmarked 4×4 route.

10.5 Another unmarked junction. Stay right, traversing west over an open meadow.

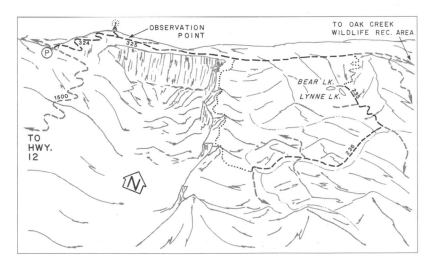

11.3 The 4×4 route traverses around the head of Oak Creek Basin. When the road begins to descend toward an open ridge on the south side of the basin, turn uphill onto the well-defined 4×4 trail, heading up the grassy slopes to the ridge. Once on the ridge (actually a shoulder of Bethel Ridge), go uphill, pushing or carrying your bike. The 4×4 trail ends immediately, but don't worry, the way is obvious and the cliffs on the west side of the ridge act as a guide. When you reach a dense grove of trees, work your way around on the west side.

12.8 The ridge tops off on Bethel Ridge at 6,000 feet. Leave the edge of the cliffs and head straight across the meadow which covers the round knoll. When you reach the trees you should find a rough 4×4 track which leads to Spur Road 325.

13.0 At Spur Road 325, go left and cycle back along the cliff to Observation Point.

15.1 Descend Spur Road 324 back to Bethel Ridge Road No. 1500.

17.2 You made it—congratulations!

If transportation can be arranged, pack a big lunch and cycle the 22 miles down Bethel Ridge on a one-way trip that ends at the Oak Creek Wildlife Recreation Area Headquarters on Highway 12.

Awesome vista from summit of Bethel Ridge

38. Pickle Prairie Adventure

Loop trip: 12.3 miles
Elevation gain: 1,300 feet
Map: Green Trails: Rimrock
Best: mid-July–September
Allow: 3–4 hours

Description: road (well maintained); trail (steep, rough, with route-finding problems)
Rating: skilled
Info: Naches RS

The Pickle Prairie Adventure is a great ride. The first time around the loop is the hardest, since numerous intersections and spur trails force you to pay more attention to route finding than to the riding or the scenery. The second time you can really let go, enjoying the challenge of the trails while riding by walls of columnar basalt, large meadows, and beaver ponds. Riders in the early morning and late afternoon have a chance to see elk, deer, coyote, beaver, and waterfowl.

The loop route is composed of three trails strung together by a couple of easy-to-ride roads. Selective logging, cat tracks, 4×4 trails, and a confusing jumble of cow paths have cut the trails to shreds. The Forest Service has attempted to mark the trails with white diamonds, but there aren't enough markers to cover all the twists and turns. So enjoy the challenge, wish yourself good luck before starting, and leave plenty of extra time for route finding.

Access: Drive 17.5 miles east from White Pass on Highway 12 (or 17.8 miles west from the junction of Highways 12 and 410).

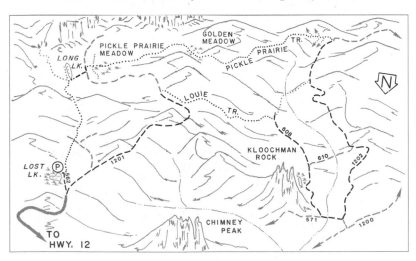

Kloochman Rock

Turn south on Tieton Road for 0.2 mile and then left on Forest Road 1201 for 4.7 miles. At the end of the pavement go left on Spur Road 562 for 0.2 mile to Lost Lake and park (3,770 feet).

MILEAGE LOG

0.0 Ride back down Spur Road 562.

0.2 Turn left on Road 1201 and cycle up, contouring above the basalt mass of Kloochman Rock.

2.3 Louie Trail No. 1126 (4,180 feet) crosses the road. Turn right and head down on the trail. Stay to the right as the trail passes through a small clump of trees and merges with a well-trampled cattle trail.

2.4 Cross the access road to the Louie Reseeding Orchard. Continue straight, paralleling the main road.

2.5 Directly below a small open area, the trail turns into a road.

2.6 Follow the road until it makes a sharp turn to the left. At this point head off the road to your right and continue down the trail.

2.9 In the middle of a long traverse, leave the trail and head left, down an old 4×4 trail.

3.2 The trail ends at an abandoned logging road. Go right and continue descending.

3.6 Pass by the edge of a large meadow and marsh.

4.3 Intersection and a choice. If you are tired of rough 4×4 trails you may take a shortcut by going left on 4×4 Route No. 610. In 0.1 mile you will intersect Road 1202. Go left and head uphill for 2 miles to the Pickle Prairie Trail, shaving 3.3 miles off the loop total. The loop route continues straight ahead on 4×4 Route No. 608, which descends along the base of Kloochman Rock and past a small beaver pond.

5.2 Turn left on well-traveled Spur Road 571 for 0.3 mile (3,000 feet).

5.5 Spur Road 571 ends. Go left and pedal uphill on Road 1202.

7.2 Pass Louie Trailhead on the left; at this point you are opposite the meadows passed on the way down. Continue up the road.

8.5 Opposite a large horse corral, turn off the road and head up Pickle Prairie Trail No. 1125 (3,780 feet). *Note:* The trailhead sign was missing in 1994. This trail is as difficult to follow as the previous one, so use white diamonds and horse tracks as guides.

8.7 The trail divides; stay right. A few hundred feet farther, the trail divides again. Take the middle trail. The next time it divides, go left and descend.

9.1 The trail descends to a small meadow. Go right and prepare for a very steep climb as the trail unites with a 4×4 route. At the top, leave the 4×4 route and follow the trail over a small ridge, descend, then go right, heading into Golden Meadow. Traverse around the meadow, then push the bike up several extremely steep hills to Pickle Prairie Meadow.

10.4 Cross a logging road.

10.8 The Pickle Prairie Trail ends at Road 1201. Go left for 15 feet, then take the first right. Cycle up to a parking area and then continue on over a small hill to Long Lake (4,300 feet).

11.1 Pass Long Lake shelter, then turn left on Trail 1145 to Lost Lake.

11.9 Cross a logging road.

12.3 The trail and loop end at Lost Lake.

Now wasn't that the kind of ride you'll remember fondly . . . in a couple of months? When it comes to recommending this trail to other people, your mother-in-law or someone who owes you money would be a good bet.

HIGHWAY 12—EAST

39. Divide Ridge

Dome Peak

Round trip: 13.0 miles
Elevation gain: 2,291 feet
Map: Green Trails: Rimrock
Best: July–mid-October
Allow: 4–5 hours
Description: ORV trail (steady climb); 4×4 road (good condition)
Rating: skilled
Info: Naches RS and DNR (Ellensburg)

Ridge Loop

Loop trip: 18.5 miles
Elevation gain: 3,091 feet
Map: Green Trails: Rimrock
Best: July–mid-October
Allow: 6–7 hours
Description: ORV trail (steady climb); 4×4 road (rough, steep); road (good condition)
Rating: adventurous
Info: Naches RS and DNR (Ellensburg)

Divide Ridge has it all: meadows and views on one side, cliffs and views on the other, and exciting riding in between.

The trip is difficult. The ORV trails are steep and the 4×4 routes are rough. Two routes are suggested here. The first is the Dome Peak ride, which follows the crest of Divide Ridge to the peak, then returns by the same route—an exhilarating descent. Riding the Ridge Loop offers a different sort of fun, with the challenge of route finding and negotiating very steep 4×4 routes and steeper cattle tracks. The final leg of the loop is on the Pickle Prairie Trail, a fun but difficult ride with several sections of walk-and-push (see Route 38).

Access: Drive east on Highway 12 from White Pass 17.5 miles, then turn right on Tieton Road. In 0.2 mile go left on Forest Road 1201. Drive 4.7 miles to the end of the pavement, then continue on another 2.7 miles. At 7.4 miles from the Tieton Road take a left on a rough, unmarked spur road, located 15 feet before the unsigned Pickle Prairie Trail. Either park here on the wide shoulder or, if you have a tough vehicle, drive up the spur road for 0.1 mile to a large parking area (4,300 feet).

DOME PEAK MILEAGE LOG

0.0 Cycle up the narrow road from Road 1201, passing the parking lot then climbing over a low hill before descending to Long Lake and a camping shelter.

0.3 Just past the shelter is a trail junction. Cycle straight ahead on Louie Way Trail No. 1126, go over a short, steep hill, then wind through the forest.

0.6 The trail starts its push to the ridgetop. Your trail is intersected several times by 4×4 routes. At all junctions continue up on the most direct route to the ridge crest.

1.1 Louie Way Gap (4,800 feet). The trail ends at a 4-way junction.

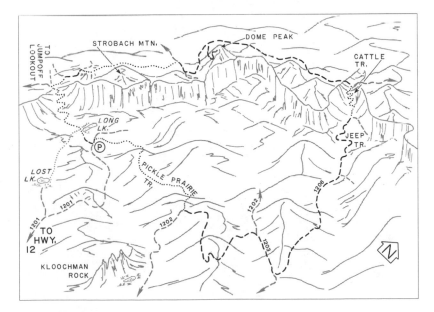

Go right on 4×4 Route No. 613. **SIDE TRIP:** To the left 4×4
Route No. 1127 climbs 2.3 miles to Jumpoff Lookout.

1.6 Take advantage of a nearby logging road to leave the 4×4
route and continue your uphill grind on a reasonable grade.

1.9 Ride around a ridge. When the road makes a sharp bend to
the right and begins to descend, find a trail on your right
and head up.

2.6 The trail levels off in open meadows on the ridge crest.

3.6 Reach open and nearly level meadows at the top of a rounded
hill (6,200 feet). The trail stays in meadows as it contours
around Strobach Mountain.

4.1 The trail intercepts the South Fork Cowiche Jeep Road and
ends. Turn right on the 4×4 route. The road heads toward
the north side of the ridge and divides; go left. Descend along
the roller-coaster crest of the ridge, then climb back to open
meadows before descending again to the base of Dome Peak.

5.9 Turn right on Dome Peak Road (6,260 feet) for the final push
to the summit.

6.5 Dome Peak summit (6,591 feet). If you have not already been
view gazing, now is the time to take it all in. The Cascade
Mountains from Mt. Stuart to Mt. Hood are spread out all
around you. Below is Rimrock Lake, and to the west lie the
Goat Rocks and Mt. Rainier. North is Bethel Ridge, to the
east is the Yakima Basin, and to the south Mt. Adams fills
the sky. Don't worry, you will have a chance to see all these
views again on the way back down.

Intersection of 4×4 trails on Divide Ridge

Kloochman Rock and Rimrock Lake from Divide Ridge

RIDGE LOOP MILEAGE LOG

0.0 Follow the Dome Peak Mileage Log for the first 6.5 miles to the summit of Dome Peak, then descend 0.6 mile back to Divide Ridge.

7.1 Turn right and descend the jeep route along the crest of Divide Ridge.

8.7 At the end of the descent is a small saddle (5,830 feet). At the lowest point of the saddle, find a well-worn cattle trail on the right-hand side of the road, heading into the trees. Follow this trail across the saddle to a narrow, rocky gully cutting down through the cliffs. Strap on your parachute, throw your bike over your shoulder, and follow the cow path down. Cross the stock fence and slide down the loose slope, still on the cattle trail, to a basin a few hundred feet below. On the bench at the upper end of the basin is a very rough 4×4 route. Follow the 4×4 route down through larch forest. The route is rutted and difficult to ride.

9.5 The 4×4 route crosses an unknown trail and continues on down.

10.2 4×4 Route No. 641 ends at Forest Road 1206 (4,760 feet). Cycle right, heading down the easy grade for 4.8 miles.

15.0 Road 1206 ends (3,560 feet). Go right on Road 1203 and start to gain back the elevation you just lost.

15.8 Road 1203 ends (3,700 feet). Cycle left on Road 1202.

16.3 Head right (uphill) on Pickle Prairie Trail No. 609 (see Route 38 for directions).

18.5 The Pickle Prairie Trail ends at Road 1201. Descend 15 feet to the start.

HIGHWAY 12—WEST

40. Packwood Lake

Round trip: 8.0 miles
Elevation gain: 71 feet
Map: Green Trails: Packwood
Best: May–October
Allow: 2–3 hours

Description: road (level, rough); trail (wide)
Rating: moderate
Info: Packwood RS

Packwood Lake lies nestled among forested hills at the edge of the rugged Goat Rocks Wilderness. It's a large lake with good fishing holes, views of lofty peaks, and a striking resemblance to any popular city park in Seattle. On a summer weekend the lake trail is crowded with hikers, pack animals, and motorcycles of all descriptions. At the lake, space is at a premium. Arrive early to stake out a picnic site and earlier still for a campsite. Once at the lake,

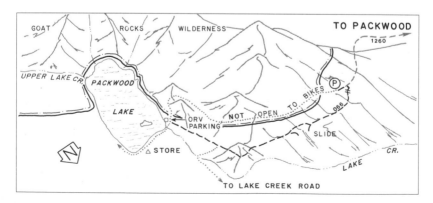

Rental boats at Packwood Lake

amenities of all sorts are available—cold drinks, hot drinks, junk food, canned food, firewood, and boats to rent.

Access: Drive Highway 12 to the east end of Packwood, then turn south on Snyder Road (Forest Road 1260). Drive past the Packwood Forest Service office, then climb steeply for 5.8 miles to the end of the road at the Packwood Lake Trailhead parking lot (elevation 2,800 feet).

MILEAGE LOG

The official hiking trail to Packwood Lake starts at the parking lot. This trail dodges in and out of the wilderness and is closed to mountain bikes. Directly below the parking lot is the water pipeline road. This road goes almost all the way to the lake and is open to cyclists.

0.0 Descend back down Road 1260 for 0.1 mile.

0.1 Turn right on the water pipeline road (No. 066). Cycle around the gate and follow the rough road on a level traverse east. On a clear day Mt. Rainier stands proudly to the north.

1.5 The road divides. Take the right fork and climb over the top of a slide.

3.0 The road divides. On the left a shortcut trail climbs up from Lake Creek Road. On the right an abandoned logging road rambles through a small clearing and over a hill, then descends to the lake. The best riding lies straight ahead, on a trail that parallels Lake Creek.

4.0 A very steep ascent up a cement path leads to Packwood Dam and the motorcycle parking area (2,871 feet). Lock your bikes here and proceed on foot. (The trail is open to mountain bikes for another 0.5 mile on the lakeshore; however, it's a very busy trail, unsuitable for riding.) Once your bike is secured, walk 50 feet out to the lakeshore and go left for 0.2 mile to the Packwood Store and boat rental. Continuing on another 0.2 mile, you'll come to a large camp area, picnic site, and trail intersection. Trail 78, on the left, heads uphill and enters the Goat Rocks Wilderness in less than a mile. The lakeshore trail enters the wilderness in 0.5 mile.

HIGHWAY 12—WEST

41. Burley Mountain

River to Pinto Rock

Round trip: 33.4 miles
Elevation gain: 6,710 feet
Map: Green Trails: McCoy Peak
Best: July–September
Allow: 7–8 hours
Description: road; steep, well maintained
Rating: skilled
Info: Randle RS

Lookout to Pinto Rock

Round trip: 18.6 miles
Elevation gain: 2,900 feet
Map: Green Trails: McCoy Peak
Best: July–September
Allow: 4–5 hours
Description: road; well maintained
Rating: moderate
Info: Randle RS

Try to describe Burley Mountain and your superlative-laced sentences string on for miles. So rather than bore you with so many words I'll stick to the barest essence of this wonderful area: a lot of climbing, a lot of views, and a lot of huckleberries, in season.

This ride has two very distinct parts. The first is a knee-creaking 8.5 miles of solid up, gaining 4,110 feet of elevation. At the top is Burley Mountain Lookout, a goal well worth the climb. The second part of the ride follows a ridge crest south from the lookout to the Pole Patch berry fields, to the French Buttes with views into the crater of Mount St. Helens, and finally to Pinto Rock, a towering rib of sculptured rock.

The recommended method for riding Burley Mountain is to start at the Cispus River and pedal (the River to Pinto Rock ride).

However, if the climb to the lookout seems a bit much, consider abusing your car rather than your knees and driving the first 7.4 miles (the Lookout to Pinto Rock ride).

The entire Burley Mountain Road is ignored by the general public, except during a few short weeks around Labor Day when the huckleberries are ripe. At that time the roads and meadows are crawling with pickers and their cars and dogs. For best riding, avoid the berry season. On the other hand, for some of the largest and sweetest huckleberries in the state, go when the berries are ripe.

Access: Drive Highway 12 to the center of Randle and go south on combined Forest Road 23 and 25. After 0.9 mile the road divides; go left, following Road 23 for 8.1 miles. Turn right on Road 28 heading towards Cispus Center. In 1.5 more miles, take a right on Road 76. Drive 3.3 miles and then turn left on Road 7605 to Burley Mountain (the turnoff is poorly signed). The gate at the base of Road 7605 is rarely closed and the only parking site lies just beyond (1,200 feet).

LOOKOUT TO PINTO ROCK MILEAGE LOG

Drive up Road 7605 to the saddle and junction at 4,800 feet, following the directions in the River to Pinto Rock Mileage Log. Start riding at 7.4 miles (trip mileages are in parentheses).

RIVER TO PINTO ROCK MILEAGE LOG

0.0 The road starts right out climbing steeply. Not to worry, the first mile is the worst. Clearcuts may open views in the future. As of 1994, the views were nonexistent.

5.7 Pass the Burley Mountain "Hikers Only" trail on the left (4,000 feet).

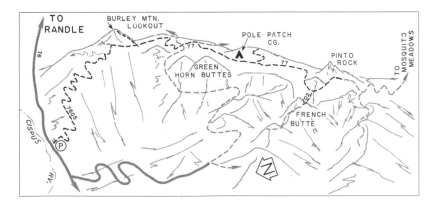

Mt. Rainier from Burley Mountain Road

6.3 First views. Burley Mountain Lookout is visible above. To the west is Strawberry Mountain Ridge.

6.4 A spur road on the left goes to a small spring. You would have to be real thirsty to drink the water. (Don't do it.)

7.4 **(0.0)** Saddle and junction at 4,800 feet. Go left toward the lookout. For those folks whose cars managed it this far, this is the start of the Lookout to Pinto Rock ride; park at the junction well off the road and cycle up to the lookout.

8.5 **(1.1)** Burley Mountain Lookout (5,310 feet). The four big snow cones (Rainier, Adams, St. Helens, and Hood) stand above an absolute proliferation of ridges, peaks, and lesser mountains. After you have rested and fully enjoyed the view, descend back to the saddle and junction.

9.6 **(2.2)** Back to the junction. Go left and descend south, heading toward Pole Patch. The descent is rapid and steep.

11.5 **(4.1)** The descent ends on a narrow saddle with a 4-way junction (4,080 feet). Road 7605 ends. Continue straight ahead, following the ridge on Road 77, a wider forest road.

11.9 **(4.5)** The improved road branches left; stay right on now-dusty Road 77, heading up.

13.8 **(6.4)** Pass Pole Patch Campground (no drinking water) and continue climbing along a steep ridge into the huckleberry fields.

14.5 **(7.1)** Pass a spur road on the left (4,700 feet) that wanders through the Pole Patch area for about 1.5 miles. The road is great for views and even better for berries. The main road climbs a little more, makes a short descent, then resumes climbing, now heading up the French Buttes.

16.2 **(8.8)** When you pass Spur Road 201 on the right you will have reached the highest point of your climb up the French Buttes (5,000 feet). Spur Road 201 can be followed to the actual 5,396-foot summit of the buttes. However, just 10 feet beyond is Spur Road 202, which offers excellent views of Mount St. Helens, without the climb. Road 77 now descends.

17.8 **(10.4)** Pinto Rock marks the end of the ride south. Stop at the 4,570-foot turnout at the southern end of the towering rock formation. A trail climbs up from the turnout for an inspection tour of the base of the rock. The road continues on down for 2 more miles to Mosquito Meadows, and meets Road 28 at 4,000 feet. The meadows are not very pretty and Road 28 takes a long time to get back to the Cispus River, so turn around and head back up.

HIGHWAY 12—WEST

42. Bishop Ridge Loop

Loop trip: 16.9 miles
Elevation gain: 3,810 feet
Map: USFS: Randle RD
Best: mid-July–September
Allow: 4–6 hours

Description: ORV trail; quality varies from excellent to extremely steep and rough
Rating: skilled
Info: Randle RS

This is not a trip for everyone. The loop ride spends its entire 16.9 miles on trails. Some of these trails are excellent, smooth, and well graded. Other trails on this loop are steep and rough.

Unless you have just brought home a yellow jersey from a renowned European road race, plan to spend at least 3 miles of the loop just walking beside your two-wheeled buddy while gaining a substantial portion of the 3,810 feet climbed on this loop.

The rewards for all your efforts to reach the crest of Bishop Ridge are numerous. You will pass a scenic subalpine lake, ride through beautiful alpine gardens, and find views of deep valleys, snow-capped mountains, and endless green hills. However, your greatest reward is a long, exciting descent back to the valley floor.

A couple of quarts of water and a large quantity of high-energy food are basic survival gear for this long ride. If you have the inclination and a license, strap a fishing pole onto your bike.

This route follows ORV trails throughout; however, hikers and horse riders also use these trails so caution is required. Make noise at all corners and slow down when you cannot see the trail ahead.

Access: Drive Highway 12 to the center of Randle then turn south on combined Forest Road 23 and 25. At 0.9 mile the road divides; stay to the left on paved Road 23 and follow it for 12.9 miles to the Bishop Ridge Trailhead (1,380 feet). The trailhead is somewhat hidden in the bushes and difficult to spot when you are driving south. Parking is limited to one or two cars on the west side of the road and to one or two cars on the east side.

MILEAGE LOG

0.0 Bishop Ridge Trail No. 272 begins by heading up through a beautiful fern grotto. After 300 feet you will reach an intersection with Valley Trail No. 270. Go right and head up the Cispus River Valley, climbing steadily along the green slopes of the hillside.

0.5 Intersection; the Bishop Ridge Trail goes left and continues

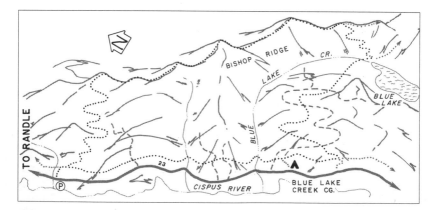

its climb. You will return to this point on the way back. For now continue following the Valley Trail (1,780 feet).

The Valley Trail heads up the Cispus River Valley, sometimes climbing, sometimes plunging downhill. Views are limited to occasional brief glimpses of the river and Tongue Mountain across the valley. The trail is fun and very rideable, except for a few, short, but very steep, pitches as it passes from cool forested glades to dusty clearcuts.

Cloudy day view over North Fork Cispus River Valley

2.0 The trail crosses a logging road. A second logging road is crossed at 3.0 miles.

3.2 Ahead is a road and huge pile of gravel. The trail goes right, descends the road for 10 feet, then heads back into the forest.

3.4 Cross Blue Lake Creek on a sturdy bridge.

3.8 Cross a logging road.

4.1 Trail 270A to Blue Lake Creek Campground branches off to the right.

4.5 Pass a trail to the Blue Lake ORV Trailhead.

4.6 Leave the Valley Trail and head left, uphill, on Blue Lake Ridge Trail No. 271 (2,050 feet), beginning the long climb out of the valley.

4.9 The trail crosses a logging road. The same road is crossed at 5.3 miles and a spur is crossed at 5.6 miles.

6.2 The relentless climb relents at last (3,500 feet) and the trail starts on a long contour around the top of a huge clearcut.

7.4 Intersection; cross Blue Lake Hiker Trail No. 274 and continue up the forested valley.

7.6 Blue Lake ORV parking (4,100 feet). Park your bike here and walk the final 100 feet to the shore of Blue Lake. If you carried your fishing pole with you, this is a great place to linger. Otherwise, take a short breather then continue on.

The trail divides at the upper end of the parking area;

stay to the left and follow Jump-Off Trail No. 271A on a steady ascent to the crest of Bishop Ridge. If that yellow jersey in your closet isn't too dusty, you should be able to pedal at least half of this next section.

8.9 The Jump-Off Trail meets Bishop Ridge Trail No. 272 and ends (4,930 feet). Also ending here is the wide, smooth tread. Go left and ride northeast along the ridge crest through meadows covered in alpine flowers. After an initial short climb, this trail is very rideable.

9.7 Cross the loop's 5,190-foot high point.

9.8 Stop on an open saddle for a view over the North Fork Cispus River Valley.

10.5 Riding becomes difficult as the trail weaves along the rocky rib at the crest of the ridge for 0.2 mile. (The trail may be

Bishop Ridge Crest

rerouted through this very difficult section in the next few years. For now the rocks serve as a barrier which discourages most motorcycles and their riders.)

11.3 The trail crosses along the top of a logging clearing (4,940 feet).

11.7 After traversing above a second clearcut there is a steep climb (push) back to the ridge crest and views over the Cispus River Valley, Tongue Mountain, and the Dark Divide.

12.3 The trail begins a definite and final descent (4,720 feet). The tread is rough with plenty of rocks to keep a check on your speed.

13.4 The trail smooths out and the descent becomes clean and fast. Watch for hikers and horses. Keep your eyes on the trail ahead, and slow down and make plenty of noise at all blind corners.

16.4 The Bishop Ridge Trail joins the Valley Trail. Go right and continue downvalley.

16.9 The Bishop Ridge Trail leaves the Valley Trail and descends a final 300 feet back to Road 23 to end the loop.

HIGHWAY 12—WEST

43. Valley Trail—North and South

North Loop

Loop trip: 11.7 miles
Elevation gain: 900 feet
Map: USFS: Randle RD (trail not shown)
Best: June–September
Allow: 3–4 hours
Description: ORV trail (some steep sections); road (paved)
Rating: skilled
Info: Randle RS

South Loop

Loop trip: 18.1 miles
Elevation gain: 1,400 feet
Map: USFS: Randle RD (trail not shown)
Best: June–September
Allow: 3–4 hours
Description: ORV trail (some route-finding problems); road (paved)
Rating: skilled
Info: Randle RS

The Valley Trail is a ride that flows to two wildly different musical themes. With a flick of a shift lever you will go from a quiet sonata to heavy metal madness as the peaceful trail leaves the fern-covered forest and drops straight down a clearcut hillside.

Soon you will be screaming around sharp switchbacks and preparing for a knee-breaking assault on the next hill.

The Valley Trail was designed for trail bikes (motorcycles) as a connector between the main routes in the Blue Lake area. Mountain bikers who love to ride trails will find this is an enjoyable ride on its own without connecting to any of the other trails in the area.

Because the Valley Trail is 15.6 miles long, it is divided here into two parts. If you are either unusually dedicated or usually crazy (or have two cars at your disposal) you can ride the entire trail in one day.

Access: Drive Highway 12 to Randle. At the center of town turn south on combined Forest Road 23 and 25, signed to Mount St. Helens. After 0.9 miles the road divides, go left on Road 23 and follow it for the next 16.2 miles to the Blue Lake ORV Trailhead, located on the left side of the road (1,970 feet).

NORTH LOOP MILEAGE LOG

0.0 This loop begins by following the trail downvalley then returns on paved Forest Road 23. From the parking area, ride the steadily climbing Blue Lake Trail up the forested hillside.

0.1 Intersection; go left on Valley Trail No. 270. The trail dips, climbs, and dives along the forested hillside and across the

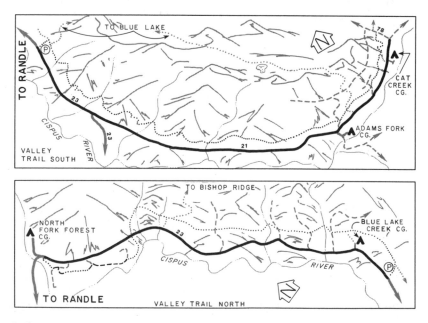

occasional clearcut. Forget about the views for now and concentrate on enjoying your ride.

0.5 Trail 270A branches off to the left, descending 0.5 mile to Blue Lake Creek Campground.

0.8 The trail crosses a logging road. You will cross a second road at 1.5 miles, a third at 1.6 miles, and, if you are still counting, a fourth at 2.6 miles. Near 3.5 miles look left for a view of the Cispus River and Tongue Mountain.

3.8 During a long sonata, the Bishop Ridge Trail merges with the Valley Trail. Continue downvalley.

4.2 The trail divides, with the Bishop Ridge Trail branching off to the left and descending to Road 23. Go straight, across a wooden bridge and continue your assault on fun.

4.4 The Valley Trail crosses the paved Road 23. Use caution when crossing. From this point on the trail is maintained by ORV clubs. The tread is rugged, and signs are lacking at many intersections.

4.9 The trail skirts the edge of the Cispus River then enters an unofficial camp area which is criss-crossed by roads and trails. Follow the road that is closest to the Cispus River and head downstream.

5.6 After passing several campsites the dirt road you have been following reaches Road 23 and ends. About 10 feet before the pavement, find an unmarked road on your left and follow it back towards the river.

5.7 The road ends at a campsite where you will find the unmarked trail.

6.4 The trail turns into a well-abused road. Continue straight on the road for a few turns of the pedal to a "T" junction. Go left.

6.5 When the road bends to the left, look for a trail on the right. This part of the trail has been signed in the past; however, the sign was mistaken for a deer, shot, tied on to someone's car, and carried home to be eaten—I guess. Follow the trail through the forest along the North Fork Cispus River.

6.7 The Valley Trail reaches Road 23 opposite the North Fork Forest Camp. The trip back upvalley may be made easily by following Road 23 for 5 miles to the trailhead or made challenging by returning by trail.

11.7 If you rode Road 23 back to the trailhead you are now back at your car sipping a cool one.

SOUTH LOOP MILEAGE LOG

0.0 The south loop begins by heading upvalley on paved roads and following the Valley Trail on the return. Start your loop

Valley Trail—South

by heading down to Road 23. Go left and settle down for a
long, steady grind upvalley.

1.9 The road divides; go left and continue uphill on paved Forest Road 21 (2,001 feet), following signs to Packwood.

8.6 The pavement ends (2,834 feet). Continue on a few feet to
an intersection where you will leave Road 21 and go left on
Cat Creek Road No. 78.

8.8 Valley Trail No. 270 begins on the left side of the road opposite the Hamilton Butte Trail. Now the fun begins. The southern section of the Valley Trail is wide enough for ATVs. The
tread is smooth with sections of soft sand. Intersections and
junctions are rare and well signed so all you have to do is
concentrate on having fun.

9.5 Pass the connector trail to the Cat Creek Campground on
the left.

10.4 The Valley Trail is bisected by Blue Lake Ridge Trail No.
271. Go straight through this intersection and continue down
the valley.

11.1 Cycle straight across a logging road. Adams Fork Campground is located just down the hill to the left.

12.5 A clearcut offers a rare view of the Dark Divide area to the west.

17.9 Blue Lake Ridge Trail No. 271 heads uphill to the right. Slow down now and in a couple of hundred feet prepare for a left turn to return to the parking area.

18.1 The Blue Lake Ridge Trail and the South Loop end at the parking lot.

44. Hamilton Buttes Loop

Road Loop

Round trip: 16.4 miles
Elevation gain: 2,100 feet
Map: Green Trails: Blue Lake
Best: July–September
Allow: 5–6 hours
Description: road (well graded, with one steep and rough section)
Rating: moderate
Info: Randle RS

Trail Loop

Round trip: 13.0 miles
Elevation gain: 2,466 feet
Map: USFS: Randle RD
Best: July–September
Allow: 3–4 hours
Description: road (part well graded, part very steep and rough); ORV trail (excellent condition)
Rating: skilled
Info: Randle RS

Some riders feel that the best time to cycle the Hamilton Buttes Loop is July through mid-August, when traffic is light. Other riders prefer late August through September, when the buttes are covered with ripe huckleberries (and people picking them). If you choose the later time, carry a container to collect a few berries of your own.

No matter what month you choose, the Hamilton Buttes Loop offers views and great riding. Two loops are suggested here, a loop entirely on forest roads and a loop that follows roads all the way up then descends on a wide, scenic, and beautifully constructed ORV trail. Optional, but strongly recommended for both loops, is a side trip on a jeep road and trail to the site of the old Hamilton Buttes Lookout.

Access: Drive Highway 12 to the center of Randle, then head south towards Mount St. Helens on combined Forest Road 23 and 25. After 0.9 miles the paved road divides; take the left fork, Road 23, and follow it for 18.1 miles. At the intersection of Roads 21 and 23 go left on Road 21 for 6.7 miles to the end of the pavement. Park in the large, informal camping area on your left (2,834 feet).

ROAD LOOP MILEAGE LOG

0.0 From your parking spot, ride up Road 21 for a few feet then go left on Cat Creek Road No. 78.

0.2 Pass the Hamilton Buttes Trail on your right and the Valley Trail on the left. Trail Loop riders will return to this point on their descent. For now stick with Road 78 and continue the steady climb, passing numerous spur roads and crossing Cat Creek several times. The climb is constant, not steep, and heads up towards a wide saddle at the north end of the Cat Creek drainage. Film-burning views of Mt. Adams appear near the top.

5.0 At the south end of the saddle, pass the Blue Lake Trailhead. Continue north into the saddle area.

5.2 Turn right on Road 7807 (at 4,200 feet) and cycle up through a large clearcut towards Mud Lake and Hamilton Buttes.

7.1 At the top of the ridge, in the midst of huckleberry bushes, is an intersection (4,900 feet). The Road Loop route continues straight ahead on Road 7807, descending east across the open hillside. **SIDE TRIP:** On the right, Spur Road 029 leads to Mud Lake and the Hamilton Buttes Lookout site. To reach Mud Lake, cycle a few hundred feet up Road 029 to a parking area and walk 0.1 mile down to the pretty little lake. To reach the lookout site, from Road 7807 cycle up Spur

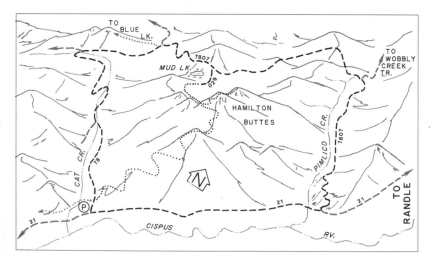

Opposite: *Mt. Adams as seen from Cat Creek Road*

Summit of Hamilton Butte

Road 029. After 0.3 mile the road is closed to further car or jeep use. Continue on up for 0.4 mile to an intersection on the ridge crest. Go left and ride or push the final 0.6 mile to the site of Hamilton Buttes Lookout (5,756 feet). The lookout was removed in the 1960s but the views remain—Rainier, Adams, St. Helens, and Hood, as well as miles of buttes and ridges that will require a very detailed map to identify. When tired of views and in need of more huckleberries, head back down to Road 7807.

10.4 At the east end of the buttes, the road divides. Take the right fork and descend down Pimlico Creek. The road is rough, with sections of uncrushed gravel to hold the sandy hillside in place.

13.1 Road 7807 ends (3,200 feet). Turn right on Road 21 and continue the descent in a more gradual fashion.

16.4 The junction of Roads 21 and 78 marks the end of the loop.

TRAIL LOOP MILEAGE LOG

0.0 Follow the Road Loop Mileage Log for the first 7.1 miles to the top of the ridge (4,900 feet).

7.1 Go right on Spur Road 209. Cycle past the Mud Lake parking area and follow the rough road up the hill.

7.4 Cars and jeeps cannot proceed beyond this point. Continue up the steep road.

7.8 At 5,300 feet the road reaches the crest of the ridge and an intersection. At this point take time for a 0.6-mile side trip to the old lookout site at the summit of Hamilton Butte. When you have returned to this point cross over the ridge and follow Hamilton Butte Trail No. 108 down the other side. After an initial switchback the trail heads into a long, nearly level traverse across a lupin-covered hillside.

8.8 The trail begins a well-graded descent.

9.1 Slow down as you pass though an open meadow for the most incredible view.

12.3 The trail divides; go left and continue to descend.

12.8 The trail ends at Road 78. Go left and descend on the road.

13.0 The intersection of Roads 78 and 21 marks the end of the loop.

HIGHWAY 12—WEST

45. Blue Lake Ridge Loop

Loop trip: 17.3 miles
Elevation gain: 3,100 feet
Map: Green Trails: Blue Lake
Best: mid-July–mid-October
Allow: 5–6 hours

Description: road (well maintained); ORV trail (narrow and steep in sections)
Rating: skilled
Info: Randle RS

This route is the best road and trail loop in the entire Gifford Pinchot National Forest. It's a surprisingly scenic ride that climbs out of the Cispus River valley to ridgetop viewpoints where Mt. Adams fills the southern horizon. The route passes pocket-size meadows, dark forest, cheerful little creeks, and one medium-size lake.

The first 6.3 miles of the loop are on well-maintained forest roads which receive only occasional use (except in late August when the huckleberries are in season). The remaining 11.4 miles are on trails used extensively by ORVs on the weekends. The trails are in fair condition; however, in some sections the soft soil has been deeply rutted by motorcycles. A couple of short, but very steep climbs will force all but the strongest riders to push their bikes.

The trails are at their best in early July when the soft soil is still damp and compact.

Access: Drive Highway 12 to the center of Randle, then head south towards Mount St. Helens on combined Forest Road 23 and 25 for 0.9 mile. When the road divides, go left and follow the paved Road 23 for 18.1 miles. Go left on Forest Road 21 for 5.5 miles to the Blue Lake Ridge Trailhead. Park in the two-car turnout on the right side of the road (2,800 feet).

MILEAGE LOG

0.0 From the trailhead, cycle northeast, up paved Road 21.

0.6 Pass Cat Creek Campground (very small and informal).

1.2 Turn left on Road 78 and begin the gradual climb out of the Cispus River valley. The road heads up the Cat Creek drainage to a broad saddle.

6.3 As the road enters the saddle, find Blue Lake Butte Trail No. 119 on the left (4,300 feet). Follow this trail across a clearcut then steeply up a forested ridge.

7.3 The steady climb ends (4,900 feet) and the trail begins a rolling traverse.

9.9 The Blue Lake Butte Trail ends (4,600 feet). Go left (south) on Blue Lake Ridge Trail No. 271. (Blue Lake lies 1.5 miles north of this intersection and almost 800 feet lower. The forested lake is an excellent objective if you are carrying a fishing pole.)

10.1 In the middle of a small meadow, ride straight across a jeep road and soon after head up and over a low, forested ridge.

11.3 Begin descent into the Mouse Creek drainage (4,900 feet).

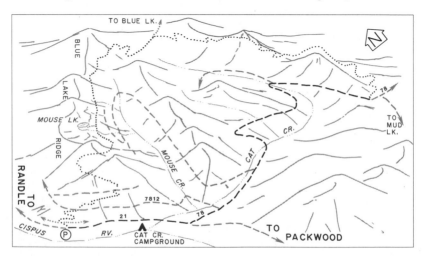

12.9 Mouse Lake intersection (4,500 feet). To reach the forested lake, go left for 0.1 mile along the outlet stream on a wide spur trail.

13.8 Begin the final descent (4,800 feet) down the steep hillside on long well-graded switchbacks. Watch out for the corners, which are tight and covered with loose rocks.

15.0 Cross a logging road.

16.1 Cross Road 7812.

Bear grass lines the Blue Lake Butte Trail in early June.

17.1 Cross Valley Trail No. 270 and continue down. This final section of trail receives little use and is quite narrow.

17.3 The loop ends on Road 21. Use caution at the end of the trail; stop and listen before crossing the road.

46. Squaw Creek Trail Loop

Loop trip: 10.4 miles
Elevation gain: 2,100 feet
Map: Green Trails: Blue Lake
Best: July–mid-October
Allow: 3–4 hours

Description: road (well maintained); trail (steep and rutted in some sections)
Rating: skilled
Info: Randle RS

Take one large forest, toss in a ridge trail with views of every Cascade volcano from Mt. Rainier to Mt. Hood, add logging roads with views of velvet-green valleys, and a side trip to a beautiful subalpine lake. Shake gently for 10 seconds, let set in your mind for 1 minute, and you are ready to ride the Squaw Creek Trail, the perfect recipe for a great afternoon.

The Squaw Creek Trail Loop is a road and trail ride. The loop starts on road, switches to trail, then finishes with more road. The trail receives most of its use from motorcycles and the soft pumice soil has been deeply rutted by the churning wheels in some sections, adding to the difficulty of the ride.

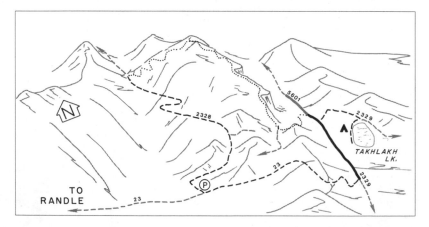

Opposite: *East Canyon and Mt. Adams*

Access: Drive Highway 12 to the center of Randle, then go south on Forest Road 23 for 28.9 miles. Turn left on Road 2328 and park (3,600 feet).

MILEAGE LOG

0.0 From the Road 2328 intersection, ride up Forest Road 23. This is a mainline route through the Gifford Pinchot National Forest, so expect traffic. The road is wide and climbs briskly.

2.9 The road divides; go left on paved Forest Road 2329 (4,320 feet) and head north across a high, thinly forested plateau.

3.7 Intersection; continue straight ahead on Road 5601. *SIDE TRIP:* Road 2329 turns left for 1 mile to Takhlakh Lake (4,444 feet). The view of Mt. Adams from the Takhlakh Lake Campground is well worth the extra effort, and the cool lake water is very beneficial to overheated cyclists.

3.8 Go left on the unsigned Squaw Creek Trail No. 265 (4,300 feet). The trail climbs for the first 0.5 mile and then drops like a rock. Watch out for patches of soft, sandy trail. In late summer, also watch for the common variety of the blue-mouthed berry picker, who comes popping out of the huckleberry bushes when least expected.

4.9 A few feet after the trail resumes climbing it reaches an abandoned logging road. Go right (uphill) and follow the road for 150 yards back to the trail. The trail enters the forest and settles into a steady climb up East Canyon Ridge. Before long you will be climbing an open ridge with views that encompass Mt. Rainier, Mt. Adams, Mount St. Helens, and Oregon's pride and joy, Mt. Hood.

6.2 The trail crosses over a forested 4,780-foot knoll then rolls west along the crest of East Canyon Ridge.

7.3 Head steeply down through forest. Motorcycles have cut a deep trough in the center of the trail. Considerable caution must be used to avoid catching a pedal.

8.1 The trail pops out onto a forest road (3,950 feet). Turn left and cycle 50 feet up to Road 2328. Go left for a leisurely traversing climb east, followed by a steep descent back to Road 23. *ALTERNATE ROUTE:* You may dramatically enlarge the loop by going right on Road 2328 for 1.4 miles. Pick up Squaw Creek Trail again in a large clearcut and descend to Road 2322 (2,400 feet). Go left, ride out to Road 23, and follow it back up to the start. There are few views and about 15 more miles on this route.

10.4 The loop ends at the intersection of Road 2328 and Road 23.

47. Pack Forest

Basic loop: 10.3 miles
Elevation gain: 1,214 feet
Map: Pack Forest Map
Best: March–mid-November
Allow: 2–3 hours

Description: road; well maintained
Rating: moderate
Info: Pack Forest

Pack Forest is an outdoor forestry lab and experimental station for University of Washington students. It is a busy lab with a working forest where the trees range from seedlings to venerable giants. Students learn all aspects of the forestry business here, from planting to harvesting. There are nurseries, demonstration plantations, and experimental areas where trees from other areas of the world are tested and grown.

A confusing network of roads loops around the forest. The loop described here is just a basic one that attempts to reach the forest's major points of interest and viewpoints without wandering in more than one circle. Roads come and go in the forest. In 1995, all the roads on the loop were in good condition.

The roads in Pack Forest are open to public vehicles on weekdays until 4:30 in the afternoon. On weekends and evenings and during hunting season, the entrance is gated and only non-motorized use is permitted.

The Pack Forest staff is happy to provide maps to visitors on

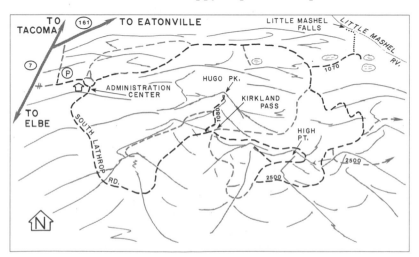

Pack Forest

weekdays when the office is open. If planning to ride on a weekend, obtain a map ahead of time by writing the University of Washington Pack Forest at 9010 453rd Street East, Eatonville, WA 98328. Let them know that bicycling is the object of the trip so that the proper maps are sent.

Access: Drive Highway 7 south from Tacoma or Highway 161 southwest from Eatonville to Highway 7. From the Highway 161 junction, go south on Highway 7 for 0.4 mile, then turn left to Pack Forest. Park in the Hiker's Parking Area (820 feet). (If you want an idea of the terrain for the ride ahead, stop at the entrance and walk through the scale model of the forest.)

MILEAGE LOG

0.0 Cycle back out of the Hiker's Parking Area and go left, up the main road towards the Administration Center. Climb a short, steep hill to the work sheds and administration buildings. The road divides; go left.

0.3 The loop begins at a "Y" intersection; go right on South Lathrop Road, heading towards Hugo Peak. The road barely gets going when it arrives at a 4-way intersection. Stay with South Lathrop Road, the upper one on the right. The road now climbs steadily, passing a nursery, two side roads on the right, and one side road on the left.

2.3 Kirkland Pass (1,580 feet). Go left on Road 1080, following signs to Hugo Peak.

2.5 The road divides; go right.

2.7 Summit of Hugo Peak (1,740 feet). Below lies the town of Eatonville and to the west you can see the southern end of Puget Sound.

3.1 Return to Kirkland Pass. In 200 feet the road divides in three directions. Take the center road and head uphill.

4.1 The High Point (2,034 feet). In the forest on the right are the foundations of an old fire lookout tower.

4.3 Leave the main road and ride the right fork out along the ridge to views of Mt. Rainier.

4.5 Check out the viewpoint and acid-rain test station, then return to the main road.

4.7 Back on the main road, go right, heading downhill.

5.0 Intersection; go left on Road 2500 and continue downhill.

5.9 Road 2500 goes right; stay left and continue descending.

6.2 Intersection; stay left.

7.3 Go right on Road 1070 for an exploratory trip to the ponds and a waterfall. The road heads straight to the entrance of a large tree plantation. At the plantation entrance, go left along the fence.

7.7 At the first corner after the plantation entrance, an old, overgrown road heads off on the left. With or without the bike, descend to the railroad tracks and walk 100 feet to the left. Just before a bridge, descend on a rough path to pretty Little Mashel Falls. Back from the falls, continue on the road for 0.1 mile past two overgrown little ponds to reach two large fish and frog ponds.

Do the bunny hop!

8.1 Back on the main road, it's a gently rolling descent past a spur road to an abandoned reservoir and 27 Creek.
9.5 The road divides; go left.
9.8 The road divides again; go right this time, on Lathrop Drive.
10.0 The loop returns to the Administration Center; go right to descend back to the parking area.
10.3 Hiker's Parking Area and end of the loop.

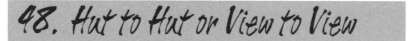

48. Hut to Hut or View to View

Loop trip: 18.3 miles
Elevation gain: 3,520 feet
Map: USFS: Randle RD
Best: mid-June–September
Allow: 3–5 hours

Description: road (steep but well maintained); trail (one very short section)
Rating: moderate
Info: Mt. Tahoma Ski Trails Association

A series of gated roads leads the cyclist on a marvelous journey along clearcut ridgetops to incredible views of Mt. Rainier and joyful descents through cool green forests. Along the way, pass two public huts which are open year-round as overnight shelters. Designed as ski shelters, these huts have great views but are located miles from water. For more information or overnight reservations contact the Mt. Tahoma Ski Trails Association, P.O. Box 206, Ashford, WA 98305.

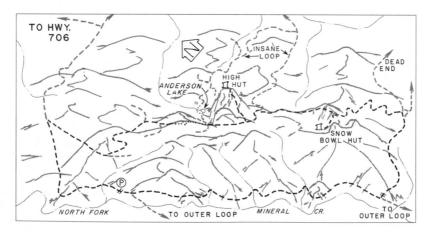

Access: From the junction of Highways 7 and 706 in Elbe, drive east on Highway 706 toward Mt. Rainier for 6.7 miles then turn right on a road signed "South District Access." Follow this rough road for 1.8 miles to a "Y" junction then go right and cross the Nisqually River. At 2.9 miles from Highway 706 the road arrives at a "T" junction. Go right and head uphill. After 2.4 miles the road divides; continue straight ahead on the #2 Road for another 2.4 miles to a Sno-Park and a gate (2,240 feet).

MILEAGE LOG

0.0 From the #2 Road Sno-Park ride back the way you came.

2.4 Go right on the #23 Road (the junction may be signed to Anderson Lake or it may not). The #23 Road climbs steeply as do all roads in the DNR system, bringing to mind a new name for the DNR roads—**Darn Near Ridiculous.**

4.0 Pass a Sno-Park parking area and continue to climb.

5.1 Reach an unsigned "Y" junction and go right. In 0.1 mile you will arrive at a second "Y"; go left.

5.6 The road ends at a large ridgetop parking area. Bounce over the berm at the far end and continue straight ahead on a cat road (4,130 feet).

5.7 Follow a well-graded trail that heads up the hillside on your left. The route is unsigned but well marked with blue diamonds.

A cloudy day at High Hut

A partly cloudy day at High Hut

6.2 The trail ends on a logging road. At this point you have two choices. The truly insane will want to take a left and head down the impossibly steep trail to Anderson Lake. You will then smash and bump around the lake's west shore to cross the outlet in 0.3 mile. Ascend a cat road to an outhouse where you will find a logging road that heads over a saddle and up to a ridgetop. After 3 miles of descending and ignoring numerous spur roads you should arrive at a well-signed intersection near the #1 Road Sno-Park. Go right, following signs for the Outer Loop Trail and High Hut, and climb 1,480 feet in the next 2.7 miles.

Normal, well-adjusted people will skip Anderson Lake. From the end of the trail go right for 20 feet then take an immediate left. The road crosses a saddle above Anderson Lake then makes a nearly level traverse around a clearcut hillside. Your route is marked with orange-tipped posts and blue diamonds.

6.8 Go left and chug up the steep road to High Hut (the insane loopers who descended to Anderson Lake will rejoin the rest of us at this point). On the way up you will pass the High Hut Loop Trail on the right; this is an alternate trail to High Hut. Ignore this trail and continue up.

7.8 The road ends at 4,760-foot High Hut. The major feature here is the view of Mt. Rainier which dominates the northeast horizon. Picnic tables on the front yard make excellent lunch spots. When you have consumed a goodly supply of carbohydrates, head back downhill.

8.8 Intersection; go left and continue the descent.

9.3 When you reach a 3-way junction on the crest of the ridge, take the right fork, following the Outer Loop Trail signs. The road descends briefly then makes another DNR climb.

10.6 Intersection; 0.4 mile to the right is the Snow Bowl Hut. Its location is pleasant but the views are not as expansive as those found at High Hut. Your route is to the left on a road that descends steeply.

11.6 The steep descent ends at a "T" junction (3,640 feet). Following signs for the Outer Loop, go right. Pass a spur road to the left then settle into a relaxing downhill glide through lush green forest.

13.8 Pass a gate and in 200 feet arrive at another "T" junction. Stay right on the Valley Trail. There are no views here so you can concentrate on a great descent. ***ALTERNATE ROUTE:*** If you would like to extend your ride, go left at the intersection and continue to follow the Outer Loop Trail adding 4.5 miles to your day's total.

18.0 The Outer Loop rejoins the Valley Trail. Continue straight down the valley.

18.3 A gate signals the end of the loop at the #2 Road Sno-Park.

MT. RAINIER—WEST

49. Westside Road

Round trip: 18.4 miles
Elevation gain: 1,680 feet
Map: Green Trails: Mt. Rainier, West
Best: July–September

Allow: 3–4 hours
Description: road (good condition)
Rating: easy
Info: Mt. Rainier NP

It was the wandering dispositions of two creeks, the Tahoma and the Fish, that finally convinced the National Park Service at Mt. Rainier to close the Westside Road to motor traffic and turn it into a hiker, biker, and horse route along the west side of The Mountain.

The result of continuing floods and washouts from Tahoma and

Fish Creeks is an 18.4-mile round trip mountain bike ride on an excellent old dirt and gravel road grade. Along with an occasional view of Mt. Rainier you will find wildflowers, forest, and creeks. If you park your bike you may take a short walk to a waterfall or an old ranger's cabin. With a bit more time, you may walk to a lake or a fire lookout. Of course if you brought your backpack with you, and have a overnight permit, you can head out on a several-day excursion along the Wonderland Trail.

Access: From Elbe drive east on Highway 706 for 13 miles to the Nisqually Entrance of Mt. Rainier National Park. Once past the entrance booth continue up the park road for 1 mile then go left on Westside Road. During the winter and spring the road is gated near the intersection. Throughout the summer the road is open to car traffic for the first 3 miles to a trailhead near the Fish Creek washout (2,860 feet).

MILEAGE LOG

0.0 Maneuver your bike over, under, or around the gate; then head up the road. When passing hikers make sure that they are aware of your presence so as to avoid collisions or scaring someone.

0.3 Cross Fish Creek on a rough and narrow rebuilt section of road.

0.6 A short section of pavement has been set into the road to aid with an unbridged creek crossing.

1.3 An unsigned trail heads upvalley along Tahoma Creek.

2.2 Tahoma Vista; the road makes a wide loop here before continuing to climb. A short stroll leads to the old and somewhat overgrown vista point.

3.6 Round Pass (3,790 feet) and time for a breather. On the left

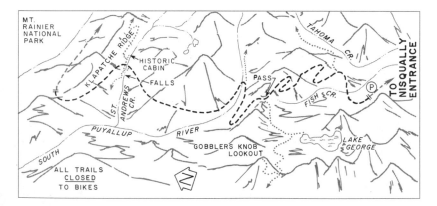

St. Andrews Ranger Station

side of the road is the Lake George–Gobblers Knob Trailhead. A bike rack here attests to the popularity of this trail, which climbs 1 mile to the lake then continues on another 1.5 miles to an outstanding view of The Mountain from the lookout on Gobblers Knob (5,500 feet). On the right side of the road a rough and nearly impassable trail descends to the South Puyallup River. Please remember that all trails in the National Park are closed to bicycles. Just beyond the trailheads is the Marine Memorial and an excellent view, weather permitting, of The Mountain.

From Round Pass, Westside Road descends through forest, passing creeks and forest wildflowers.

5.0 Pass the South Puyallup Trailhead, which offers access to the exquisite Emerald Ridge in just 3.3 miles.

6.2 The road begins to climb again.

7.9 St. Andrews Creek bridge (3,800 feet). On the left side of the road at either end of the bridge is a 0.2-mile trail to the Denman Falls viewpoint. The falls is especially scenic in the early summer. Once across the bridge you will pass the trails to the St. Andrews Ranger Station (located 300 feet from the road) and to the beautiful Klapatche Park (2.5 miles)

Denman Falls

and the high alpine St. Andrews Lake (3.3 miles). Beyond the bridge the road continues to climb.

9.2 Klapatche Point (3,990 feet) is the current official end of Westside Road and turnaround point for this ride. From this point you may continue by foot for 2.7 miles to the former end of Westside Road and the Wonderland Trail.

CAPITOL FOREST

50. Capitol Peak Loop

Loop trip: 21.8 miles
Elevation gain: 2,328 feet
Map: Capitol Forest Recreation Map
Best: April–October
Allow: 6–7 hours

Description: road (steady climb, well maintained); ORV trail (some rough sections)
Rating: skilled
Info: DNR (Chehalis)

Capitol Peak + capital views = capital road-and-trail riding.

We are now going to study the above equation. Pay attention—there will be a field exam after the lecture.

Capitol Peak is the highest summit in the Black Hills (a group of very green hills located at the southern end of the Puget Sound basin). The view from the summit of Capitol Peak is worth an entire chapter in a geography textbook. To the north the saltwater channels, bays, and mud flats that mark the southern terminus of Puget Sound are visible. There is a grandstand view to the east spanning the Cascade Range from Mt. Baker to Mount St. Helens. To the northwest the Olympic Range fills the horizon and to the west lies the greatest landmark of them all, the Pacific Ocean.

The peak is part of the Capitol Forest Multiple Use Area operated by the Department of Natural Resources (DNR). The main use of the forest is logging, and the secondary use is recreation. As a result the hills are laced with logging roads and trails.

This loop uses roads to take you up to the summit of Capitol Peak and trails to bring you back down. Expect a moderate amount of traffic on the roads at all times and heavy traffic during hunting season. The heaviest ORV use is on summer weekends. The trails are usually closed to motorcycle use from November 1 to March 31. (These dates vary from year to year depending on how wet the trails are.)

Access: Take Exit 95 off Interstate 5 and drive 3 miles west on

State Route 121 to the town of Littlerock. Drive straight through town. Leave State Route 121 when it turns left, and continue west 0.7 mile to a "Y" intersection. Take a right on Waddell Creek Road for 3.9 miles to Yew Tree Campground. Go left, into the camp area, and park (330 feet).

MILEAGE LOG

0.0 Before cycling back to Waddell Creek Road, take a look at the creek and decide whether or not you wish to ford it at the end of your loop.

0.1 Turn left on Waddell Creek Road.

0.4 At a paved 3-way intersection, go left.

1.8 The pavement ends and the road divides. Go left on C-Line Road and, following the signs to Capitol Peak, begin to climb.

3.8 Pass a shortcut road to Capitol Peak on the right. (This road is much steeper and 3 miles shorter.) A few feet farther, the road to Falls Creek branches off on the left.

8.8 C-Line Road reaches the ridgetop and ends. Go right on Road C4000 and cycle along the western side of Black Hills Crest. Below, views extend over rolling fields, past two cooling towers left over from the abandoned WPPSS project, to the shining waters of the Pacific Ocean.

11.3 The road splinters into three parts. Go straight, on the steep road in the middle, climbing the last hill to the summit of Capitol Peak. (The road on the right is the upper end of the shortcut road.)

11.5 Summit of Capitol Peak (2,658 feet). The summit area looks

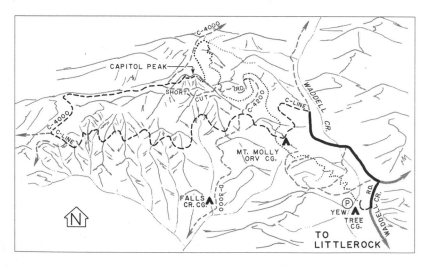

Beauty and the beast

as if it was taken over by aliens. It is bristling with relay towers and windowless cement buildings. Look past the structures to find the best lunch spot on the twin summits.

To descend, cycle to the east side of the highest summit and head down a steep jeep road. In 150 feet go right on a wide ORV trail. Use caution here, as there are a lot of loose rocks.

11.9 The trail crosses the jeep road. Go straight, heading north.

12.6 The trail and road come together (2,280 feet). Do not cross the road. Continue straight, contouring below Larch Mountain.

13.2 Trail intersection (2,240 feet). Go right, heading down on smooth, well-graded trail.

13.4 A confusing junction (1,950 feet); slow down or you may find yourself on the wrong trail. Take the upper trail on the right-hand side (Trail 40), and head back to the south following the contours of the hillside.

15.3 The trail crosses the shortcut road (1,880 feet) and, 100 feet beyond, crosses a steep jeep road. Go straight.

17.8 The trail ends temporarily on the shortcut road (1,270 feet). Go left, uphill, for 200 feet, then take a right back onto the trail.

19.2 Cross C-Line Road.

19.5 The trail traverses around the right side of Mt. Molly ORV Campground.

19.6 The trail crosses a road, then heads steeply up through a clearcut.

20.1 Cross a logging road at the upper end of the clearcut, then head back into the trees. Here the trail divides; go straight ahead.

20.2 The climb ends at the top of a 1,160-foot hill.

20.7 The trail divides; stay left.

21.0 Cross an unmarked trail and continue the descent down a clearcut. A few feet beyond, cross another logging road and continue down.

21.4 The trail crosses a well-traveled road. If Waddell Creek looked too deep to ford, go left here and descend to Waddell Creek Road, then right back to Yew Tree Campground. If the creek was low enough to cross, continue straight for another 0.2 mile, then take the first well-used trail on the left.

21.8 Yew Tree Campground and end of the loop.

CAPITOL FOREST

51. Rock Candy Mountain Loop

Loop trip: 17.6 miles
Elevation gain: 1,924 feet
Map: Capitol Forest Recreation Map
Best: April–October

Allow: 5–6 hours
Description: ORV trails; well maintained
Rating: skilled
Info: DNR (Chehalis)

The Rock Candy Mountain Loop is a place to watch the seasons change. Ride here in early spring to catch a glimpse of the first yellow skunk cabbage or tender alder leaves. In early summer you'll find trillium and dogwood in bloom. Fall brings a kaleidoscope of colors as the leaves burn with fiery hues. In early winter you may ride over a carpet of leaves and mud puddles rimmed with ice.

The loop follows well-maintained ORV trails for most of the distance. The heaviest ORV use is on summer weekends. To protect the area from excessive erosion, the trails are usually closed to motorcycles. (These dates vary from year to year depending on how wet the trails are.)

Access: Take Exit 95 off Interstate 5 and drive 3 miles west to the town of Littlerock on State Route 121. Drive through town, leaving State Route 121 when it turns left. Continue straight for 0.7 mile to a "Y" intersection. Go right on Waddell Creek Road and drive for 4.3 miles to a large, paved intersection. Take a left and head west for 1.3 miles to a "T" intersection then turn right on Noschka Road for 1 mile to Bordeaux Camp. Park here (440 feet).

MILEAGE LOG

0.0 At the southwest side of the camp area, a wide ORV trail heads into the trees. Cycle up this steep trail and, when it divides, stay left.

0.1 The trail meets a road—turn right. After 20 feet, find the trail on your left, heading uphill.

0.2 The trail from the campground ends. Go right on Trail 1, which winds along the forested hillside with a breathtaking series of ups and downs.

1.1 The trail ends on a logging road. Go left and cycle up the valley on the road.

1.6 Cross a creek on the road bridge, then go right, back onto Trail 1. The trail heads up the valley following the route of an abandoned road which, due to speeding motorcycles, undulates like ocean waves.

2.5 The trail turns right, leaving the old road and crossing Waddell Creek on a log bridge.

3.4 Cross a second creek and begin to climb a series of rideable switchbacks.

5.4 The trail ends on a forested ridgetop (1,400 feet). Go left on

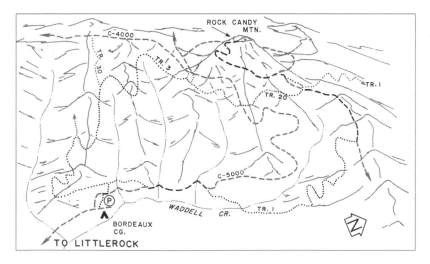

Waddell Creek bridge

an abandoned road that tunnels through walls of second-growth forest and salal.

6.8 A 4-way intersection (1,715 feet). The loop route goes left; however, as no views bless this otherwise perfect ride, a 2.6-mile round trip to the summit of Rock Candy Mountain is a must. From the intersection, take the right-hand trail for 10 feet, then go left on an overgrown trail heading steeply uphill.

7.0 The trail ends. Go right and follow the road 0.1 mile up to a wide intersection. Turn left here and cross a dip pit dug to keep 4×4s out. Your route follows an old railroad grade toward the summit. View starts immediately, with a broad vista north over Summit Lake, the southern bays of Puget Sound, and the Olympic Mountains. Near the top the road deteriorates, and you may have to push.

8.1 Rock Candy Mountain summit (2,364 feet). Gaze over an outstanding view that includes Mt. Rainier, Mt. Adams, and Mount St. Helens.

When you leave the summit, head back the way you came 1.3 miles to the 4-way intersection.

9.4 Back at the 4-way intersection, go straight.

10.2 The trail crosses a road (from Bordeaux Camp) and heads back into the forest to continue its traverse south (1,680 feet).

11.6 Poorly marked intersection (1,560 feet); continue straight ahead for 500 feet to a second intersection. Once again go straight on Trail 3, which continues to contour south for 2 miles before descending.

14.9 Trail 3 is joined by Trail 30 from Larch Mountain (1,210 feet). Continue straight ahead, heading down rapidly.

16.7 The trail divides near Noski Creek (700 feet). Go left, away from the creek, following an old railroad grade.

17.4 A "T" intersection marks the end of the loop. Go right, following the trail back to the camp.

17.6 Bordeaux Camp.

CAPITOL FOREST

52. Zig Zag Loop

Loop trip: 22.3 miles
Elevation gain: 1,070 feet
Map: Capitol Forest Recreation Map
Best: March–November

Allow: 5–6 hours
Description: road (nearly level); ORV trail (well graded)
Rating: skilled
Info: DNR (Chehalis)

The best description of mountain bike riding in Capitol Forest is fun. The ORV trails are wide, with banked corners for exhilarating descents and graded to allow the energetic cyclist to ride

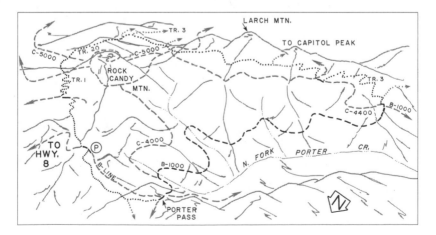

up as well as down. Areas exist where cyclists can find better views, but no area in the state has as wide a selection of fun trails as Capitol Forest.

The Zig Zag Loop is just one of the many fun rides starting from the Rock Candy Mountain Entrance. It's a road-and-trail ride. The road portion is on old railroad. The trail portion includes climbs, rolling traverses, and a thrilling mile-long descent on the Zig Zag.

Traffic on the forest roads is generally light except during hunting season. The heaviest ORV use on the trails occurs on summer weekends. To protect the area from excessive erosion, the trails are usually closed to motorcycles from November 1 to March 31. (The dates vary from year to year depending on how wet the trails are.)

Access: Drive Interstate 5 to Exit 104 in Olympia. Go west on Highway 101 North for 6 miles. When Highway 101 heads north, stay to the left on Highway 8 for another 4.6 miles. At the top of a long hill, turn left on Rock Candy Road and enter Capitol Forest. In 0.2 mile the road divides; stay right and drive under the

Zigzag, then splash!

powerlines. Where the road divides a second time, stay right again. Following the road, pass a house, then head steeply uphill paralleling the powerlines. At 1.8 miles from Highway 8 pass a wide ORV trail on the right. Continue on for 50 feet to a large parking area on the right (930 feet). If this area is blocked, go on up the road until you find a safe pullout.

MILEAGE LOG

0.0 Cycle 50 feet back down the road, then go left on the wide ORV trail which heads up the powerline cut.

0.8 The trail crosses under the powerlines. Two roads head steeply uphill; take the second (the well-used maintenance road) and climb to the main road.

1.0 Head straight ahead through a narrow cut into the Porter Pass area (1,140 feet).

1.1 The road divides; go left, toward Bordeaux Camp.

1.6 Go right at an unsigned intersection in the middle of a large clearcut on Road B1000 and follow an old railroad grade southwest through forest and clearcuts for the next 8.5 miles.

10.1 Intersection (1,180 feet). Go left for 0.1 mile.

10.2 Turn right on a wide, unmarked ORV trail. In 100 feet reach Mt. Molly–Porter Trail No. 3. Make a sharp turn back to your left and begin the long grind over the shoulder of Larch Mountain.

12.6 The trail reaches a road, go right, up to a "T" intersection. Cycle straight across the intersection to find the trail (1,720 feet) and continue to climb.

14.5 The steady climb ends at the junction with Capitol Peak Trail No. 30 (2,000 feet). Continue straight ahead on Mt. Molly–Porter Trail No. 3, which traverses northeast around Larch Mountain.

17.9 The trail intersects a road at a 3-way (road) junction (1,560 feet). Go straight ahead and find the trail on the right side of the road intersection. In 100 feet is a trail junction. Go left, still following Mt. Molly–Porter Trail No. 3.

18.1 Intersection; go left on Trail 20. (Mt. Molly–Porter Trail No. 3 goes right.)

18.2 Poorly marked junction. Go left on Trail 20, which contours around the east side of Rock Candy Mountain.

19.6 The trail crosses Road C2100 (from Bordeaux Camp), then heads back into the forest to continue its climbing traverse (1,680 feet).

20.4 A 4-way intersection (1,715 feet). The loop route goes straight ahead on North Rim Trail No. 1. Hang on to your pedals and your brakes and head down the Zig Zag. (The trail on the left at the 4-way intersection climbs 1.1 miles to the summit of Rock Candy Mountain; see Route 51 for details.)

21.4 Go left for 100 feet on a logging road at the top of a large clearcut, then turn right, back on the trail.

21.7 The trail ends; go left on an abandoned railroad grade.

22.3 The loop ends at the edge of the powerline cut. Go left and pedal 100 feet up the road to the parking area.

MOUNT ST. HELENS

53. Marble Mountain

Loop trip: 13.2 miles
Elevation gain: 1,568 feet
Map: Green Trails: Mount St. Helens
Best: mid-June–October
Allow: 2–3 hours

Description: road; some rough and narrow sections
Rating: moderate
Info: Mount St. Helens National Volcanic Monument

This road ride is not only one of the most scenic in this book but it is also sure to rate high on the fun meter. While lacking great technical challenges, the descent on narrow, rarely used logging roads is exciting enough to put a smile on every face in your group.

Access: Exit Interstate 5 at Woodland and drive east on State Route 503 for 28.8 miles to Cougar. Go straight through town for another 6.8 miles then take a left turn onto Road 83 and head uphill for 3 miles. When the road divides stay right and drive around the east side of Mount St. Helens for the next 3.6 miles to the June Lake Trail turnoff. Go left for a final 0.2 mile and park at the trailhead (2,900 feet).

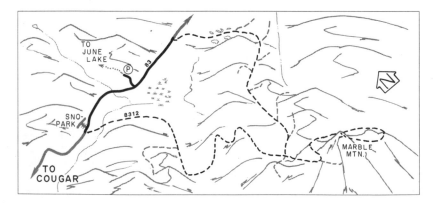

MILEAGE LOG

0.0 Follow the paved June Lake Trail access road back down to Road 83.

0.2 Turn right, heading back the way you came on Road 83, and ride the pavement for the next 0.9 mile, enjoying several great views of Mount St. Helens as you go.

1.1 Pass the gated Marble Mountain Sno-Park on the right then take the next left on Road 8312. This gravel road begins with a descent. Watch for large potholes and washboard.

1.6 The road crosses a creek (2,800 feet) then begins a steady climb up the clearcut hillside. Several spur roads are passed; stay with Road 8312. After a steady 2 miles of climbing your efforts will be rewarded by an outstanding view of Mount St. Helens.

4.3 Reach a 4-way intersection (3,450 feet). *Note:* On the way back you will start the loop portion of the ride by following the road that is now on your left. For now, go straight through the intersection and ride across a broad saddle before heading into the final ascent. Ignore all spur roads as you keep those pedals rotating. The view continues to improve as the road winds around the east side of the mountain then corkscrews back to the west side.

6.6 The good road ends at a point just below the summit. You may either leave your bike here or ride straight up a rough cat track for the final 0.1 mile to the summit.

6.7 The cat track ends at a small building (4,128 feet). Walk around the north side of the building to find a narrow trail that heads along the hillside to views and huckleberry bushes. From various points around the summit of Marble Mountain you will see Mount St. Helens, Mt. Rainier, Mt. Adams, Mt. Hood, and Mt. Jefferson. After soaking in the view head back down the same way you came up for 2.4 miles to the 4-way intersection.

9.1 At the 4-way intersection, go right. This road had a number, but brave hunters killed it. Luckily the route you will follow is a snowmobile trail in the winter and well marked with orange diamonds and black arrows. Watch for these markers as you go.

9.3 Pass a spur road on the right, then, at the next intersection, go left.

9.9 Head down through an old clearcut, passing first a spur road on your right, then one on your left, then another spur road on the right.

10.8 Just when Mt. Adams seems to fill the entire eastern horizon, go left on a small spur road.

11.2 Go left on a wider road and head west over a broad plateau, passing several small ponds.

12.0 The gravel logging road reaches pavement and ends (2,795 feet). Go left, and descend on Road 83.

13.0 Turn right and follow the June Lake Trail access road back to your car.

13.2 So which did you enjoy the most, the ride or the scenery?

Note: Although this is the only ride in Mount St. Helens National Volcanic Monument mentioned in this book, there are many others. All roads and some trails are open to mountain bikes. When riding pumice areas, please stay on the road or trail you are following. Do not venture off route on the fragile pumice or we may lose our riding privileges in this area.

Mount St. Helens from Marble Mountain Road

54. Jones Creek ORV Trails

Loop trip: 11.2 miles
Elevation gain: 2,400 feet
Map: DNR: Yacolt Burn State Forest
Best: May–October
Allow: 4–6 hours

Description: road (well-maintained gravel); ORV trails (rough, rutted, and very steep)
Rating: adventurous
Info: none

You have to be a wee bit masochistic to go trail riding on the Jones Creek ORV System. Twisting and winding through the forest at the start of the ride, you may be fooled into thinking that these trails are fun; however, it won't take you very long to discover your error. Before long you will be climbing up a trail that seems to be the shortest route to the summit of Mt. Everest. Things do not improve when you head down. Loose rubble, axle-deep ruts, and exposed cinder blocks will soon have you believing that you are descending into an abode of the damned.

All in all, the Jones Creek ORV Trails make for a glorious riding experience for those of us who cannot pass up a challenge or, because of some mental deficiency, love to brag about how many times we rolled over our handle bars in a single ride.

Note: The Jones Creek ORV area is an energy-demanding adventure through a twisted spaghetti system of unmarked trails. Be prepared to get misplaced more than once on this short loop. The trails are set up to be ridden in a counterclockwise direction. This may work on a motor-powered cycle; however, mountain bike riders will find the trails work better in a clockwise direction. As you

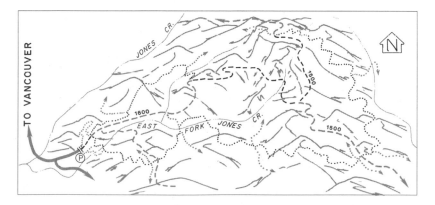

One of the small challenges riders will find in the Jones Creek ORV trails system

will be riding against the flow, you'll need to be extra courteous to the motorized trail users.

Access: From Vancouver drive Interstate 205 to the Orchards Exit then follow Highway 500 east. At the second stoplight turn right on Fourth Plain Blvd. (still following 500 East). After 6.3 miles take a left turn on 53rd Street and follow it for 3.2 miles before turning left on Ireland Road. After another 0.3 mile go left once again on Lessard Road and follow it (and signs to the ORV Trails) for 4 more miles to the large trailhead parking area (1,080 feet).

MILEAGE LOG

0.0 From the parking area start your ride by continuing up gravel-surfaced Road 1600. (You may start out on the trail from the north parking area; however, you will soon find yourself meandering through a forest where trails converge and divide like a bowlful of spaghetti. At the end of a fun, but confusing, 0.9 mile of riding you will cover the first 0.1 mile of road.)

0.1 Leave the road and go left on a well-used trail that skirts along the edge of the road then begins to climb.

0.6 The trail arrives at a "T" junction; go right.

0.9 A "Y" junction; go right and descend to cross a creek on a bridge. The trail then heads into a relatively easy rolling traverse.

1.4 The trail rolls over two rocky berms and ends at Road 1600. Go left on the road and begin a thigh-burning climb up the steep road.

2.9 Road 1600 intersects Road 1500 and ends at a 2,030-foot pass. Go left and continue climbing. (If you are not having the time of your life and would like to shorten your agony, and the ride, you may go right at the pass and follow Road 1500 over a hump then steeply down. After 1 mile watch for an unmarked trail crossing on a corner. Go right and pick up the ride description at the 6.9-mile log entry.)

4.0 At 2,440 feet the road reaches the ridge crest. The dirt has been plowed away here, leaving a wide gravel platform and a good place to stop and check out the view over the Columbia River to Portland and Mt. Hood. After you have soaked in the view, find a trail on the right-hand side of the road and head down steeply into the trees. After a screaming, 0.6-mile descent on a very rough trail, you will pass another Columbia River viewpoint.

5.7 Junction; stay right and begin wandering up and down through the forest. The ascents are short, and creek crossings are bridged, but use caution when descending exposed cinder blocks. If you spill, the cinder blocks will definitely bite back.

6.5 The trail enters a clearcut with the last views of the ride.

6.8 An unmarked trail branches off to the left. Continue straight and climb to Road 1500.

6.9 Cross Road 1500 (1,680 feet). After 50 feet your trail will cross an unmarked trail. Continue straight, descending then climbing again.

8.2 After a steep drop you should find yourself at a 4-way junction (1,760 feet). Go right for 75 feet to a second intersection then go left and head down a rutted trail marked by two posts.

8.9 Cross East Fork Jones Creek. *Note:* In 1994 a section of the bridge was missing.

9.4 At a "T" junction (1,190 feet) go left and descend to recross

East Fork Jones Creek. Just beyond the creek is a 3-way junction; go right.

10.0 The trail crosses a gravel road.

10.1 Ride straight through a 4-way intersection.

11.0 Cross a bridge and begin the final climb.

11.1 The trail reaches Road 1600 and ends. Go left.

11.2 Return to the parking area. Repair your bike and body then head out and explore all the trails you passed by on the first time around.

55. Hardtime Loop

Basic Loop

Loop trip: 10.5 miles
Elevation gain: 760 feet
Map: USFS: Wind River RD
Best: June–October
Allow: 1–2 hours
Description: roads; paved and gravel in good condition
Rating: easy
Info: Wind River RS

Extended Loop

Loop trip: 21.5 miles
Elevation gain: 2,200 feet
Map: USFS: Wind River RD
Best: June–October
Allow: 3–4 hours
Description: roads (good condition); ski trails (rough and brushy)
Rating: moderate
Info: Wind River RS

Despite the name, you will not have a hard time when riding this loop. In fact, the Basic Loop is excellent for first-time riders and for family groups.

The Basic Loop follows the forest road portion of the Hardtime Cross-country Ski Loop and finishes off with a cruise along the paved surface of Forest Road 30. Along the way you will wander through delightful forests as well as through clearcuts to find views of Mt. Adams, Mt. Rainier, and Mount St. Helens. The Extended Loop was designed for those riders who want a bit more exercise and a lot more views. The Extended Loop is the same as the Basic Loop except for an added round-trip excursion to a viewpoint overlooking Swift Reservoir and the south side of Mount St. Helens.

Access: Drive Highway 12 along the Columbia River to the Carson turnoff then head north on Highway 141. Go right on Road 30. After 11.1 miles you will cross Oldman Pass. Continue on another 0.5 mile then take a left on a paved road. Park in the large Sno-Park (2,980 feet).

BASIC LOOP MILEAGE LOG

0.0 From the left side of the parking area, ride up gravel Road 3054.

0.1 Ride around a gate and head into solitude (as long as there are no logging operations in progress in the area).

0.3 An intersection of winter ski trails is marked by a profusion of blue diamonds. Continue up the gradually climbing road.

0.6 Descend past a clearcut and enjoy your first view of Mt. Adams, peaking over East Crater and Blue Mountain.

1.4 After pedaling through a large clearcut the Scenic Loop (a ski trail) branches off to the right.

1.6 The summit of Mt. Rainier can be seen over the Dark Divide.

1.9 The truncated summit of Mount St. Helens comes into view over the crest of a forested ridge.

2.4 The road dips to cross Hardtime Creek.

4.3 The loop route leaves Road 3054 (3,250 feet) and heads off into the band of trees to the right. Blue diamonds clearly mark this junction. Walk or ride your bike across the rough area next to the road then ride over a mound of dirt. Head down a rough, narrow road that is marked with an abundance of blue diamonds.

4.7 After a bend to the left, the rough connector road ends at Road 3050. Go right and begin the best descent of the loop. *Note:* This road is not gated so watch for traffic.

7.4 Cross Hardtime Creek then cycle across a rolling plateau.

8.9 Road 3050 reaches Road 30 and ends (2,898 feet). Go right on Road 30 and cycle the pavement back to the start.

10.5 Turn right, off Road 30, and return to your starting point at the Sno-Park.

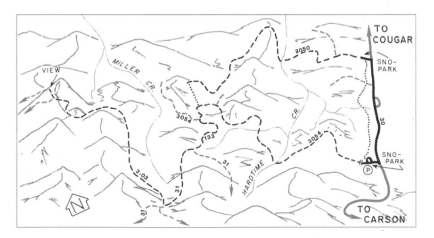

Swift Reservoir

EXTENDED LOOP MILEAGE LOG

0.0 Follow the Basic Loop Mileage Log for the first 4.3 miles.

4.3 Note where the Hardtime Loop (Basic Loop) leaves Road 3054 then continue on up, following the road over a ridge.

4.6 Soon after you cross the ridge prepare for a left turn on Spur Road 133 (3,300 feet). Spur 133 climbs steadily to views of Mt. Adams and Mt. Rainier, descends, then climbs again.

5.7 Cycle around a gate.

5.8 Spur 133 ends (3,563 feet). Go right on well-graded and frequently used Road 3100.

6.8 Turn right off Road 3100 onto less-traveled Road 3103 (3,545 feet) and start a delightfully scenic cruise along the ridge.

9.2 Intersection; go left and descend Spur Road 155 for 400 feet then go right on an unsigned road.

9.6 Stop and enjoy the view. Even though the road continues, this is a good place to turn around and head back to the Hardtime Loop.

14.9 Rejoin the Hardtime Loop by heading left on the connector trail to Road 3050.

15.3 Go left and follow Road 3050 for the next 4.2 miles.

19.5 Just before Road 3050 reaches Road 30 and ends, Snow Foot Trail No. 148 branches off to the right. This is exclusively a cross-country ski trail which receives only minimal brushing out and most riders should expect to walk several sections. Riding the Snow Foot trail is a challenging but fun way to close this loop. (If this trail does not sound appealing head back to the start on paved Road 30.)

20.0 The Snow Foot Trail crosses a road. Continue straight ahead.

20.1 In the middle of a clearing pass a trail sign. The Snow Foot Trail bends to the right.

20.8 At the edge of a forest plantation go right and head up an obscure road.

21.0 The Snow Foot Trail intersects an old road; stay to the right.

21.4 Leave the Snow Foot Trail as soon as you see the parking lot and complete the ride in grace and style, on pavement.

21.5 Loop ends.

WIND RIVER

56. McClellan Meadows Trail Loop

Loop trip: 12.6 miles
Elevation gain: 1,550 feet
Map: USFS: Wind River RD
Best: mid-June–September
Allow: 3–4 hours

Description: road (good condition); trail (rough and poorly maintained)
Rating: skilled
Info: Wind River RS

Take a romp through the forest on trails that are rarely used after the snow melts. The trails are maintained for cross-country skiing and summer users will find challenging riding over tree roots and rocks, making for a wild, zig-zaggy ride. The trail used for the ascent is gradual and moderately strong riders should be able to ride its entire length.

Access: Follow Highway 14 along the Columbia River to the Carson turnoff then head north. After passing through Carson, follow Highway 141 past Wind River then go right on paved Forest Road 30 (just past the Fish Hatchery). Continue north for 13.7 miles to find an unsigned Sno-Park on the right with a restroom, picnic table, and area map. Park here (2,904 feet).

MILEAGE LOG

0.0 Start your ride by heading up gravel-surfaced Road 3053, which begins from the north end of the parking area. This is a well-maintained road which sees little automobile use except during hunting season.

1.6 Shortly after passing McClellan Meadows the road begins to deteriorate, then soon divides into two rough spur roads. Go straight ahead on McClellan Meadows Trail No. 157, which takes off between the two spur roads and heads into the trees. This trail is well marked with signs and blue diamonds (the cross-country ski trail symbol). The climb is steady but never radically steep. However, a great deal of concentration is required to successfully weave your way over and around the rocks and roots on the trail. At the same time keep a lookout for horses, which can be occasionally encountered on this trail.

2.1 When the trail divides, stay to the left, following the blue diamonds. After 200 feet cross a small creek on a log bridge.

2.6 The trail reaches the crest of a small hill and divides; stay left. The trail will descend then cross Pete Gulch on a log bridge.

3.2 Cross Road 6701 then continue the gradual climb.

4.6 The McClellan Meadows Trail reaches Road 65 and ends (3,600 feet). Go left and continue to climb on the forest road. Watch for fast-moving vehicles along this portion of the loop. After a mile of steady climbing, Mount St. Helens comes into view sporting its crewcut and blown-out side.

7.3 When you reach a large grassy meadow watch for Snow Foot Trail No. 159 on the left side of Road 65 (4,020 feet). The

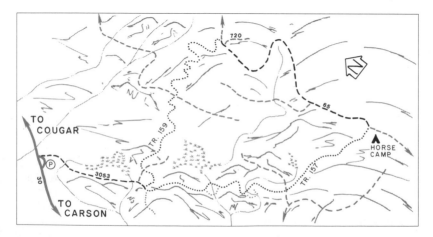

The cross-country ski trails see only light maintenance during the summer.

meadow is cut with trails and old roads so you must follow the blue diamonds carefully for the first 0.2 mile until you enter the forest. The descent is much like the ascent, on a narrow trail covered with rocks and roots. The grade is not steep; in fact, it is just perfect.

8.5 The trail enters a large clearcut and the tread is lost under a heavy mat of bear grass. Follow the blue diamond markers half way across the clearcut then head down and to the right with a couple of lazy switchbacks. If you keep the blue diamonds in view you should find a good trail when you re-enter the forest after 0.3 mile.

8.9 Cross a spur road and continue the descent.

10.9 The trail enters another large grassy clearing and once again disappears. Keep the blue diamonds in sight and continue to descend.

11.1 The trail ends at Road 3053. Go right and follow your tracks back to the start.

12.6 The ride ends at the Sno-Park. Now who said you need skis to enjoy a cross-country ski trail?

TROUT LAKE

57. The Buttes Loop

Loop trip: 15.2 miles
Elevation gain: 2,060 feet
Map: USFS: Mt. Adams RD
Best: July–September
Allow: 3–4 hours

Description: road (mixture of pavement and dirt); trail (sandy)
Rating: skilled
Info: Mt. Adams RS

Trail, 4×4 route, logging road, and paved road all play a part in this varied loop through the heartland of the Gifford Pinchot National Forest. The route passes through forests, meadows, and clearcuts to reach a topnotch view from an old lookout site on West Twin Butte.

This area is virtually ignored throughout the spring and early summer months. However, starting in late August, campgrounds,

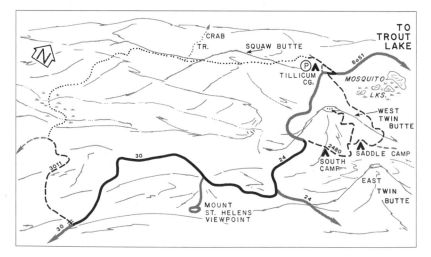

roads, and trails are inundated with berry pickers. At about the time the last berries are picked, the hunters arrive and riding here loses much of its appeal.

Access: Drive west from the town of Trout Lake on State Highway 141 for 0.7 mile to Forest Road 88. Turn right for 12.8 miles to Road 8851, then continue straight ahead for another 3.4 miles to a major intersection just beyond Big Mosquito Lake. Turn left on Road 24 and drive 1.1 miles to Tillicum Campground. Descend to the campground, then follow Spur Road 271 past the camp loop, to Squaw Butte Trail No. 21. Park here (elevation 3,800 feet).

MILEAGE LOG

0.0 Squaw Butte Trail begins with a steep climb on an abandoned road.

0.2 Leave the old road and go right on the trail, which continues the uphill grind.

1.4 The trail crosses over a forested ridge just below the summit of Squaw Butte (4,300 feet), then heads west, descending along the crest of the ridge.

1.5 Junction with Crab Trail No. 20; continue straight along the ridge.

Descending Squaw Butte

Mt. Rainier viewed from the old lookout site on West Twin Butte

4.2 The trail fords a small but rather deep creek; wade or use one of the many logs near the crossing.

4.5 Cross a second stream, on a bridge this time.

4.6 The trail enters a clearcut and follows an old cat road. The route is clearly marked with white diamonds affixed to posts along the trail.

4.8 The Squaw Butte Trail meets Road 3011 and ends (3,260 feet). On clear days look northwest over Skookum Meadows for an excellent view of Mount St. Helens, then go left and cycle up Road 3011 for 2.4 miles.

7.2 A gate marks the end of Road 3011 (3,780 feet). Turn left on Road 30 and ride on pavement for the next 2.7 miles, passing the turnoff to the Mount St. Helens viewpoint. (Cycle up to the viewpoint only if you want the exercise; better views await.)

9.9 Road 30 ends (4,080 feet). Turn left on paved Road 24 for 1.1 miles.

11.0 Turn off the pavement onto Road 2480 (4,000 feet) signed to South and Saddle Camps. The road climbs steadily up forested West Twin Butte.

11.3 Pass the turnoff to South Camp.

12.2 Just before the entrance to Saddle Camp, go left (road number was not legible in 1994). The road climbs steeply through huckleberry fields toward the summit of West Twin Butte.

13.0 The road ends (4,670 feet). Park the bike and continue on foot up a short, steep trail to the old lookout site on the 4,740-foot summit of West Twin Butte for a 360-degree view which includes Mt. Adams, Mount St. Helens, Mt. Rainier, the Goat Rocks, Sawtooth Mountain, East Twin Butte, Squaw Butte, and Bird Mountain, just to name a few. You'll also see a whole host of rolling green hills, clearcuts, and lakes. When you have had your fill of the view, return to the bike and swoosh back down to Road 2480.

14.0 Turn left on Road 2480 and descend through Saddle Camp. At the lower end of the camp, bounce over a large trench, designed to stop 4×4 traffic, and continue on down the road. Watch out for another, larger trench at the base of the hill.

14.5 Road 2480 ends. Turn right on Road 24 and ride on pavement for 100 feet, then turn left and descend back through Tillicum Campground.

15.2 The loop ends at the Squaw Butte Trailhead.

TROUT LAKE

58. Middle and Service Trails Loop

Loop trip: 20.7 miles
Elevation gain: 1,600 feet
Map: USFS: Mt. Adams RD
Best: July–mid-October
Allow: 3–4 hours

Description: roads (well maintained); ATV trails (excellent condition but lacking bridges at creek crossings)
Rating: skilled
Info: Mt. Adams RS

If you can imagine a painting of Whistler's Mother with a mustache you can visualize this road-and-trail loop. A portion of the ride follows a well-maintained road along the east side of Indian Heaven Wilderness. At the northern end of the loop the road enters the berry fields where small lakes lie in the folds of the huckleberry-covered hills and Mt. Adams dominates the eastern horizon. It is a definite classic and classy scene. The only negative note, the mustache, is the number of cars you may encounter along the road. The second half of the ride is on exquisitely designed ATV trails which have wide-banked corners and a soft tread. However, in the midst of this blissful riding experience you must be ready for several difficult, bridgeless creek crossings (the mustache again). Overall this is not a difficult ride, the roads and trails being almost too easy. So maybe Whistler's Mother does not look so bad in a mustache after all.

Note: Early-season riders should expect to wet feet at the creek crossings. Only at the end of a long, hot summer can you hope to complete this ride with dry shoes.

Access: From Trout Lake head west on State Route 141 (which becomes Forest Road 24) for 11 miles. Pass Road 8821 on the right and continue on for 0.1 mile to find a large turnout with room for three or four cars on the left side of Road 24. Park here (3,640 feet).

MILEAGE LOG

0.0 The loop starts off with a good warm-up ride on Road 24. This section of the ride heads through forest with few views. Watch for traffic.

0.9 Ride through a 4-way intersection. To the right is Road 8831, which you will cross on your way back. For now continue straight on Road 24.

1.6 Pass Smoky Creek Forest Camp.

2.7 A road sign indicates the southern trailhead of Middle Trail No. 26; continue on the road.

2.9 Road 24 passes through Little Goose Forest Camp. The horse camp is on the left and the car camp is on the right. Continue along the road as it rolls along the eastern border of Indian Heaven Wilderness. All trails passed on the left lead into the wilderness and are closed to mountain bikes.

4.4 Pass the 0.2-mile-long trail to Hidden Lakes.

5.3 After a steep descent the road passes Cultus Creek Forest Camp.

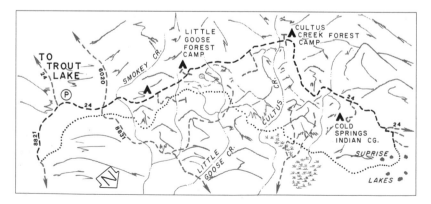

5.9 Pass Indian Viewpoint (4,000 feet), which has an excellent vista over Sleeping Beauty to Mt. Adams.

8.5 A 20-foot trail leads to an interesting historical marker at the edge of the berry fields.

8.7 Pass a turnout on the left which has a pit toilet, informational signs, and short trails leading into the Sawtooth Berry Fields.

8.9 Following signs to Middle Trail No. 26, turn right on Spur Road 230 (4,253 feet). After 150 feet the road divides; stay right. As you ride this narrow road, watch for small white diamonds which mark the trail's route.

9.1 The road divides; stay right.

9.3 The road divides again. Stay right, following the white diamonds.

9.7 The road ends. Continue on a wide ATV trail, which descends rapidly into the forest.

11.1 The steep descent ends (3,560 feet). At this point you must tackle your first ford before heading across the broad North Fork Meadow Creek marshlands.

11.3 Cross a wide bridge then prepare for a brisk climb.

11.6 The trail crosses Spur Road 100 then continues to climb.

11.8 At 3,800 feet the trail crosses Spur Road 091 then levels off in preparation for the next descent.

12.3 The descent ends at the Cultus Creek ford (3,580 feet). The rocky bottom of the creek makes for a difficult crossing.

12.8 The trail reaches a spur road and disappears. At the time of this writing you must go left about 40 feet then rejoin the trail, which reappears on the left. Expect changes here in the future.

12.9 Cross the spur road.

13.2 Little Goose Creek is crossed with a deep ford.

13.9 It takes four bridges and one ford to take you and your bike over the next swampy area.

14.8 Intersection (3,940 feet). To the right, Middle Trail heads out to Road 24. The loop route continues straight ahead on Service Trail No. 35. (Ignore the unsigned trail in the middle.)

15.0 Cross a small creek which is often dry by late summer.

16.5 The trail fords Smoky Creek then heads steeply up over a band of lava.

16.7 Stay left at a "Y" intersection.

16.9 When the trail divides, stay left a second time and ride around a clearcut and a corral.

17.0 Cross Road 1831. The Service Trail now follows the route of an old road.

17.9 Go left on an abandoned spur road and after 100 feet ride straight through an abandoned intersection.

Spur Road 230

19.2 The Service Trail meets Road 8821 and ends (3,620 feet). Go right on Road 8821 which makes a short climb before descending to Road 24.

20.6 Road 8821 ends. Go right on Road 24.

20.7 Find the turnout and your car on the left.

59. Red Mountain

Round trip: 17.4 miles
Elevation gain: 1,945 feet
Maps: USFS: Mt. Adams RD and Wind River RD
Best: mid-June–mid-October
Allow: 4–5 hours

Description: road (varying from well graded to steep and very rough)
Rated: moderate
Info: Mt. Adams RS

From small details like the whorls and twirls of lava, to larger scenes like the fascinating glimpse of an old Indian racetrack, to a huge panoramic view over the entire southern Washington and northern Oregon Cascade Range, this is indubitably the most interesting ride in the Gifford Pinchot National Forest.

Unfortunately, this ride follows a mainline forest road for part of the trip where you must constantly be on guard for fast-moving traffic. The final section of the ride is a steep climb to Red Mountain Lookout. This rough road is gated except when fire danger is high at the end of the summer.

Access: Drive west from the town of Trout Lake for 8.1 miles

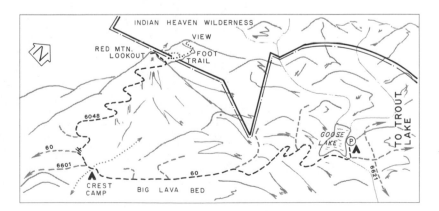

on State Route 141 (which becomes Forest Road 24). Turn left on Road 60 and follow it 5.5 miles to Goose Lake Campground. Park near the boat launch (3,150 feet).

MILEAGE LOG

0.0 Before heading out, take a good look at Goose Lake. Until the mid-1950s Goose Lake did not exist. In its place was a lava vent hole. Several small streams drained into the hole and disappeared. In an attempt to help out Mother Nature, someone decided to fill the vent hole and create a lake. Several tons of rock and dirt were poured down the hole with no effect. A few years later a beaver couple moved into the neighborhood; a year later a good-sized lake formed. The old vent is now visible only in late summer when the water level is low.

After checking out the lake, ride back out of the campground and go right on Road 60. The road heads around the

View of the Indian Race Track

northeast side of Big Lava Bed and you will see some fascinating walls of lava. Note also how the thin soil supports trees but very little underbrush.

1.2 Spur Road 220 branches off on the right.

2.1 The steady climb abates.

2.4 Pass Spur Road 241 (3,570 feet).

2.5 A small turnout on the left provides an excellent location to view the lava bed.

2.8 Pass a second turnout and lava inspection point, also on the left.

4.2 The road crosses a 3,600-foot high point then begins to descend.

4.7 Pass the primitive Crest Camp. The Pacific Crest Trail crosses the road here.

4.9 Road 6801 branches off to the left. Stay on Road 60 and continue to descend.

Goose Lake

5.2 Go right on Road 6048 (3,390 feet). Pass the gate then begin the long hard climb to the summit of Red Mountain.

5.5 About the time you pass an unmarked spur road to the left, you may crane your neck back for a view of the lookout far above.

6.1 The gravel surface ends and the road quality deteriorates.

6.3 The road briefly descends before heading into the real climb.

8.5 Indian Race Track Trail No. 171 branches off to your right. Pass it by for now and continue toward the top.

8.7 Red Mountain summit (4,965 feet). You have earned this view so sit back and enjoy it. The major peaks are easy to identify—Mt. Adams, Mt. Hood, Mt. Jefferson, Mount St. Helens, and Mt. Rainier—however, you will need a detailed map to identify the less renowned summits.

8.9 *SIDE TRIP HIKE:* Just 0.2 mile below the summit is Indian Race Track Trail No. 171. This trail is not open to mountain bikes so all explorations must be done on foot. The object of this excursion is a viewpoint overlooking a meadow that was once used by Indians for racing horses. Over time the forest has encroached on the meadows and only a short section of the racetrack is still visible. For the best viewpoint you need to walk to the top of the next knoll to the north. Just follow the Indian Race Track Trail steeply downhill for 0.1 mile to a saddle. Leave the trail and head up the loose lava to the crest and view.

17.4 The ride ends back at Goose Lake Campground.

TROUT LAKE

60. Buck Creek Trail Loop

Loop trip: 13.8 miles
Elevation gain: 1,100 feet
Map: USFS: Mt. Adams RD
Best: July–September
Allow: 3–4 hours

Description: road (well maintained); trail (well maintained)
Rating: skilled
Info: Mt. Adams RS

On the Buck Creek Trail Loop you will encounter a variety of riding conditions ranging from paved road to dusty cattle trails. The loop starts in a forested valley bottom and climbs to open clearcuts and excellent views of Mt. Adams and Mt. Hood. This is a quiet loop. The trails receive little use and the roads are rarely busy.

Access: Drive State Route 141 to the town of Trout Lake. At the southern entrance to town is a "Y" with a service station in

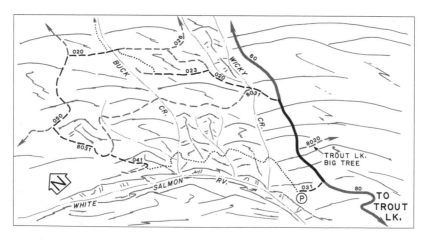

Buck Creek Trail

the center. Take the right-hand fork of the "Y" for 1.3 miles to an
intersection. Stay right for 0.6 mile then take a left turn on Forest
Road 80 signed "Mt. Adams Recreation Area." After 2.3 miles take
a left off the pavement onto Spur Road 031 and follow it for 1 mile
to the Buck Creek Trailhead (2,690 feet).

MILEAGE LOG

0.0 The loop starts by following Buck Creek Trail No. 54 on a
short descent, then traverses across a steep hillside. Several streams are crossed in this section. Major streams have
solid bridges and one minor stream may be forded or crossed
by walking a log.

0.2 Reach an unsigned "T" junction. Go right and descend to a
bridge.

0.8 The trail traverses a narrow shelf several hundred feet above
the White Salmon River. Stop and enjoy this scenic section
of trail before ducking back into the forest away from the

river. The trail climbs a small, fern-covered valley to a narrow saddle and then plunges steeply down the other side.

2.0 Dangerous hairpin turn—use caution. Shortly beyond it, the trail begins a steep climb.

2.7 The trail meets Spur Road 041 and ends (3,000 feet). Turn right and cycle up the road for 1.2 miles.

4.0 Spur Road 041 ends. Go left on Road 8031.

4.8 Turn right and pedal up Spur Road 050 (3,240 feet), enjoying some closeup views of Mt. Adams.

6.4 Take a right on Spur Road 020. On a clear day Mt. Hood will appear on the horizon at the first clearcut.

7.5 As soon as Spur Road 025 branches off on the right, start watching for a profusion of plastic tape that marks a well-used cattle trail. The trail will appear first on the left side of the road and then, about 40 feet farther, on the right. (If you reach Spur Road 026 without finding the trail, you have gone 0.6 mile too far.)

7.6 Turn right on the unsigned cattle trail (3,700 feet) and head down. The trail starts with a rolling descent through forest and ends with a plunge through a clearcut to a forest road. The major users of the trail are cattle, so watch out for these large beasts and the ever-present brown pancakes on the way.

8.3 The trail ends; turn left on Spur Road 023.

9.5 Spur Road 023 ends; turn right and descend on Spur Road 020.

10.8 Spur Road 020 ends (3,080 feet). Go left on Road 8031.

11.4 Road 8031 ends; turn right on Road 80 and descend on smooth blacktop.

12.3 *SIDE TRIP:* Go left on Road 8020 for 0.2 mile to visit Trout Lake Big Tree.

12.8 Turn right onto Road 031 for the final level mile back to the Buck Creek Trailhead.

13.8 The loop ends at the trailhead parking area.

Index

About the Author

Tom Kirkendall went on his first overnight back-packing trip at the age of three and since then has never stopped exploring the outdoors. He has logged countless miles on foot throughout the Cascades, Sierra Nevada, northern Rockies, Great Smoky Mountains, and European Alps. When summer fades into winter, he trades his hiking boots for cross-country skis, and the adventure continues. His passion for the outdoor life extends beyond the mountains to the ocean, where he spent part of his youth as an amateur competitive surfer, and to the road, where bicycle touring and racing remain a vital part of his life.

Tom lives in western Washington with his wife, Vicky Spring, and their two children, Logan and Ruth. In addition to writing guidebooks, Tom and Vicky are professional photographers, specializing in landscape, international travel, and adventure photography.

Other titles you may enjoy from The Mountaineers:

Mountain Bike Emergency Repair, Tim Toyoshima
Shows how to perform temporary trailside repairs with few or
no tools, and then make permanent repairs with proper tools.
Tips on finding post-crash problems, preventive maintenance,
the "7 essential bike survival tools."

Bicycling the Backroads ™ Series
Each provides complete directions, points of interest, terrain,
detailed mileage logs, maps, elevation profiles, and more!
> ***Around Puget Sound***, 4th Ed., William & Erin Woods
> ***Northwest Oregon***, 2d Ed., Philip Jones & Jean
> Henderson
> ***Northwest Washington***, 3d Ed., Erin & Bill Woods
> ***Southwest Washington***, 3d Ed., Erin & Bill Woods

Biking the Great Northwest, Jean Henderson
Presents multi-day tours, many of them loops, for great Northwest cycling vacations. Includes mileage logs and notes on
terrain, history, scenic highlights, cycling smarts.

Bicycling the Pacific Coast, 2d Ed., Tom Kirkendall &
> Vicky Spring
Information on road conditions, availability of provisions,
accessible campgrounds, and points of interest.

Mountain Bike Adventures ™ Series
Feature accurate route descriptions and highlight wildlife,
scenery, and historic and natural sites.
> ***The Four Corners Region***, Michael McCoy
> ***The Northern Rockies***, Michael McCoy

THE MOUNTAINEERS, founded in 1906, is a nonprofit outdoor activity and conservation club, whose mission is "to explore, study, preserve, and enjoy the natural beauty of the outdoors. . . ." Based in Seattle, Washington, the club is now the third-largest such organization in the United States, with 15,000 members and five branches throughout Washington State.

The Mountaineers sponsors both classes and year-round outdoor activities in the Pacific Northwest, which include hiking, mountain climbing, ski-touring, snowshoeing, bicycling, camping, kayaking and canoeing, nature study, sailing, and adventure travel. The club's conservation division supports environmental causes through educational activities, sponsoring legislation, and presenting informational programs. All club activities are led by skilled, experienced volunteers, who are dedicated to promoting safe and responsible enjoyment and preservation of the outdoors.

If you would like to participate in these organized outdoor activities or the club's programs, consider a membership in The Mountaineers. For information and an application, write or call The Mountaineers, Club Headquarters, 300 Third Avenue West, Seattle, WA 98119; (206) 284-6310.

The Mountaineers Books, an active, nonprofit publishing program of the club, produces guidebooks, instructional texts, historical works, natural history guides, and works on environmental conservation. All books produced by The Mountaineers are aimed at fulfilling the club's mission.

Send or call for our catalog of more than 300 outdoor titles:

The Mountaineers Books
1001 SW Klickitat Way, Suite 201
Seattle, WA 98134
1-800-553-4453